D

Microwave Cookery
by
Carolyn Dodson

"Definitive Microwave Cookery" is a brief compilation of some of her favorite recipes ... and a treasure of valuable information for both beginning and accomplished microwave cooks. Her dialogue with the reader is relaxed, easy to understand and, even better, her recipes are sure fire hits at the dinner table.

Dedication

This book is dedicated to my husband, Bill, my family and friends who acted as "tasters" during the many long hours I devoted to this book instead of them.

The Library of Congress Number TX1718604
ISBN 0-9619966-0-9
6th Printing October 1988

The Author

Carolyn Dodson is known as the leading authority and expert on in-home microwave usage and currently consults with international corporations in the areas of product development, promotion and sales. In 1985 she published her own book "Definitive Microwave Cookery."

Ms. Dodson appears regularly on television network affiliates and cable "daytime programming" in addition to providing print copy on extended microwave usage for newspaper and magazine. She has produced for television over 150 eight minute progam segments which ran during 1986.

In addition to consulting, writing and doing personal appearances on television and radio talk shows, Ms. Dodson generates large numbers of very interested attendees at Women's and Trade shows where she skillfully lectures, presents and demonstrates in-home microwave procedures, recipes and uses that take the "guess work" out of microwave cooking.

Tens of thousands of tastefully satisfied eaters have enjoyed Carolyn Dodson's convenient microwave recipes. Indeed, Ms. Dodson is the unquestioned leader for in-home microwave usage.

From Carolyn: "I'd like to get to know you and hear what you have to say about the fun, convenience and taste of microwave cooking. To help keep you current on microwave cookery as new fun ideas become available, please complete the below information and send to: Carolyn Dodson, P.O. Box 8341, Wichita, KS 67208. I look forward to receiving it."

CAROLYN DODSON'S "DEFINITIVE MICROWAVE COOKERY"

Name _____ Occupation _____

Street Address _____

City _____ State _____ Zip _____

Number of people in your household? _____ Your age _____

How did you get a copy of my book? _____

What do you think of it? _____

Favorite dishes are: _____

Would you like more information on microwave cooking? _____

GENERAL INFORMATION

HOW A MICROWAVE WORKS

The magnatron tube sends microwaves across the top of the oven where they "hit" a stirrer fan and bounce down into the oven. Inside the oven, the microwaves "bounce all around" to give us our even cooking. Microwaves are reflected off of the metal walls; they pass through the paper, plastic or glass that holds our food, like sunshine through a window, with no effect at all and the microwaves are attracted like magnets to the water molecules within the food. The microwaves penetrate the food from 1 - 1½ inches deep causing the molecules to vibrate against one another at the rate of 2½ billion times a second. This friction causes the heat that cooks our food. Heat from the vibrating molecules then moves toward the center of larger food, which cannot be penetrated by the microwaves. Therefore on larger, more dense foods, the cooking is started on the edges and the heat is conducted to the center. This is why you will find arrangement of food, dish style, denseness of food, etc. can all play an important part in microwave cooking.

TEST FOR HOT SPOTS IN YOUR MICROWAVE

Cover the bottom of your microwave with a dampened paper towel. Turn on the microwave for 1 minute at 100% power. The dried out areas/wet areas show the cooking pattern or hot and cold spots of your oven. Severe problems should be corrected by a service representative. If the hot/cold spots are not severe, learn to use these areas to your advantage. Harder to cook foods or portions of food can be placed in the hotter areas ... easily cooked portions may be placed in the cooler areas. Example: Leg of lamb roast ... place the small end of leg in the cool area; the large area of the roast in the hot area.

TEST FOR POWER FLUCTUATION IN YOUR HOME

The power supply in your home may vary throughout the day, thereby affecting your microwave cooking times. Bring a cup (same temperature) water to a boil in your oven at three different times during a day. For example: 8 a.m., 12 noon and 5 p.m. You will see that times will vary. This shows the "peak" times for power usage. This will usually be the same each day. Therefore, you may need to adjust your cooking time up or down by a few seconds to account for this. On delicate food this can really make a difference in the finished product.

CORRELATION OF CONVENTIONAL AND MICROWAVE TEMPERATURES

The scale below shows how you can learn to relate your microwave "percentage of power" to your conventional "degrees of heat."

100-90% power is equivalent to deep fat fry, broil or 500-425 degrees of heat in your oven.
80% power is equivalent to 375-425 degrees of heat in your oven.
70-60% power is equivalent to 325-375 degrees of heat in your oven.
50% power is equivalent to 300-325 degrees of heat in your oven.
30-40% power is equivalent to 300-225 degrees of heat in your oven.
20% power is equivalent to 200-225 degrees of heat in your oven.
10% power is equivalent to 150-200 degrees in your oven or as low as you can turn the burner on top of your stove without it going off.

If your microwave has its powers listed by words such as Simmer, Roast, etc., look in your owners manual as it will give you the percentages for each position. You will see that learning to relate microwave and conventional temperatures, you will be able to adapt your "conventional" recipes to microwave more easily. (See further in book on Recipe Conversion.")

UTENSILS

Microwave cooking patterns in various types of pans and proper "circle fashion" arrangement of food is demonstrated below.

Cooking patterns of different pans

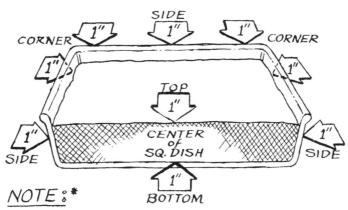

NOTE:*

Corners cook 4 ways - from 2 sides, top & bottom
Sides cook 3 ways - from 1 side, top & bottom
Center cooks 2 ways - from top & bottom only

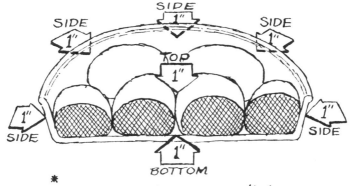

* See NOTE under square dish.

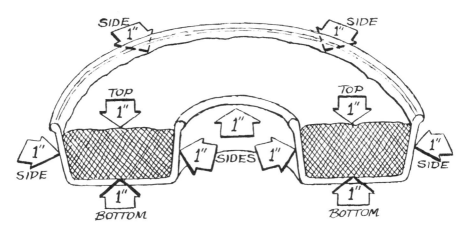

Food arrangement for even cooking without stirring or rearranging

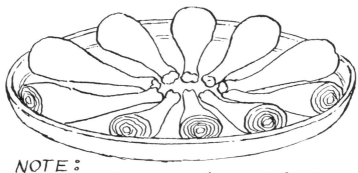

NOTE:
Place thicker portions of food
to outside of dish, thinner portions
to the center area of dish.

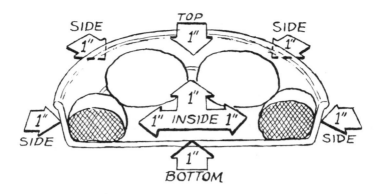

TESTING UTENSILS

Place tepid water in a styrofoam cup. Place the cup of water in the microwave and bring it to a boil (about 2 minutes at 100% power). Empty the hot water and replace with more tepid water. Place the cup of water and the dish to be tested in the oven, side by side. Turn the oven on at 100% power for the length of time it took the first cup of water to boil. After this time, the cup of water should be *very* hot or almost boiling ... the dish should be "cool" or barely warm.

If this is the case, the dish is microwave safe. If the dish is hot ... it is not good for use in the microwave.

COVERS AND LIDS

There are three basic "lids" or "covers" used for microwave cooking. They are summarized below:

Plastic Wrap
Used for recipes calling for "tightly covered", "steaming", "moist", etc.

Wax Paper
Used for recipes calling for "crack the lid", "allow some steam to escape", "partially cover", etc. You may also use your lid that belongs to the dish you may be using for this type of covering.

Paper Towels
Used for recipes calling for "dry heat", "crusty", "absorb excess moisture", "no lid", or to simply prevent splattering and hold heat.

SHIELDING

Small piece of foil may be used to cover various parts of food to keep them from overcooking. For example: The wings, breast bone and leg ends of a chicken or turkey that is being baked may get over done if not protected or "shielded" for part of the cooking time. You may also place a foil ring or "donut" over cakes, eggs, etc. for more even cooking.
(80% food volume - no more than 20% foil volume.)

STANDING TIME

Six minutes a pound at 100% power will cook most all foods to done. 80% occurs in microwave while cooking. 20% takes place after the oven turns off, whether you want it to or not. As an auto putting on its brakes and coming to a gradual stop, so the water molecules which are moving 2½ billion times a second must also come to a gradual stop. We must allow for this or foods will overcook. *I have built this factor into the 6 minutes per lb. rule. (See Meat Section, Lowering Temperatures, for more explanations.)* On meats for example, internal temperatures will raise 10 to 15 degrees. Therefore, meats will cook as follows:

	Stop Time Temperature	After Standing Temperature
Rare	120 degrees	135-140 degrees
M. Rare	125 degrees	140-145 degrees
Medium	135 degrees	150-155 degrees
M. Well	140 degrees	155-160 degrees
Well	150 degrees	165-170 degrees

"Tent" or cover meat with foil during the standing time. This helps the heat distribute evenly. Also check the temperature in several areas throughout the meat to make certain of even doneness.

DEFROSTING

Proper times for defrosting is dependent on types and sizes of food. Always cover while defrosting. The bigger the piece, the lower the temperature to prevent cooking from occurring. A very porous type of food will also defrost more easily than a dense one. As a rule of thumb, use the following chart to help you defrost:

1" thick	6 min. per lb. at 50% power
1½" - 2" thick	7 min. per lb. at 40% power
2" - 3" thick	8 min. per lb. at 30% power
3" - 4" thick	9 min. per lb. at 20% power
Over 4" thick	10 min. per lb. at 10% power

REHEATING

Reheat foods gently at 50% power according to food type. Arrange dense, hard to heat portions to outside of plate. Porous, easily heated food to the inside or center of the plate. This type of arrangement makes it unnecessary to rearrange or stir. Cover according to the texture you desire (Example: moist food-plastic wrap; medium moist texture-wax paper; dry or crusty texture-paper towel). Cook about 6 minutes per lb. at 50% power. Stir if necessary. Bottom of the plate or bowl will be warm to the touch when food is hot.

To cook or reheat TV dinners - uncover dinner and return dinner to box. Defrost for 3 - 4 minutes at 50% power. Next, cover with foil the easily cooked foods leaving the harder to cook foods uncovered. Place back in the box and cook another 1 - 2 minutes. Uncover the entire dinner and place back in the box. Finish cooking 1 - 3 minutes more until very hot. Frozen dinners or entrees may also be placed in another container to heat. If dish is more than 1" deep you must place in another container.

To reheat bread use the chart below as a guide:

Unsliced bread	1 loaf	30 seconds	100% power
Sliced bread	2 slices	10 seconds	100% power
	4 slices	20 seconds	100% power
Buns and Rolls	2	20 seconds	100% power
	4	30 seconds	100% power
Donuts	2	15 seconds	100% power
Sweet Rolls	2	20 seconds	100% power

CONVERTING RECIPES

You must adapt your recipes according to size and wattage of your oven. Cook times for various ovens are as follows for each minute cooked:

600-700 Watt Oven	500-600 Watt Oven	400-500 Watt Oven
1 min.	1 min. 15 sec.	1 min. 30 sec.

As most recipe books are written for 600-650 watt ovens, it may be necessary to adjust your cooking times by adding or subtracting necessary seconds as above for each minute you cook your food.

For example: If the 600-700 watt oven takes 1 minute to cook; 500-600 watt oven would take 1 min. 15 sec. and a 400-500 watt oven would take 1 min. 30 seconds, so adjust accordingly to allow for this time difference.

Look for recipes that will convert well. For example: Recipes that call for "moist cooking", "stirring", "covering", "steaming", "sauces", etc. will convert from conventional to microwave easily. Stay away from those that suggest "Crusty", "Golden Brown", etc. They do not convert well.

Less liquid is needed in foods (20 - 25% less) that are converted from conventional to microwave.

Butter or oils for searing and sauteing aren't needed except for flavor if desired.

Substitute quick cooking rice for converted rice.

Fat and oil may be reduced 10% — adding fats causes more intense heat and effects cooking times.

Increase leavening by 10% when baking from "scratch". Rapid cooking doesn't give leavening time to work. It is also good to let batter set a minute or two to help leavening get started.

Cornstarch sauces thicken more rapidly and need less stirring than flour based sauces.

Less spices as flavors from spices will be more intense in microwaved foods.

Stir or arrange food properly. Proper size of dish ... fit the food to the bowl size.

Cut pieces of food uniformly for even cooking according to denseness. Aside from food being dense and porous and uniform in size, another factor that presents itself in microwave cooking and the heat intensity with which it cooks is the water, sugar and fat content within each food. For example: Water heats "fast" (212 degrees); Sugar heats "faster" (260 degrees); Fat heats "fastest" (300 degrees), thereby being the hottest intensity of heat. Therefore, the content of water, sugar and fat within our foods will also affect the rate of speed and heat intensity that food will cook.

FACTORS THAT LESSEN COOK TIME: High water, sugar, oil content, small pieces, porous and tender texture, warm starting temperature.

FACTORS THAT LENGTHEN COOK TIME: Low water, sugar and oil content, large pieces, dense and tough texture, cold starting temperature.

Use similar techniques for cooking converted recipes in the microwave as you would if you were cooking the food conventionally. Ask yourself — "Do I cook this recipe on high heat?" "Do I cook this on low heat?" You would then select the suitable temperature for the type of food being cooked. Continue to ask yourself questions and compare the methods to conventional cooking methods. "Do I cook it covered?" "Uncovered", etc. Do it the same in the microwave as you would conventionally. Think conventional. Food is food, so we handle it the same way, no matter what cooking method.

Microwave cooking time should be reduced to ¼ of the conventional cooking time to begin. You may add more time if needed. For example: conventional recipe cooks for 1 hour at 350 degrees, covered. Microwave recipe would cook for 15 minutes at 70% power, covered with plastic wrap. (Refer to previous information on temperature and coverings).

MICROWAVE HINTS

1. To clean a microwave place 1 cup of water with 1 tsp. of vanilla or almond extract in the microwave. Heat for 2 minutes at 100% power. Use a dry cloth to wipe out the inside of the oven. A pleasant smell, too!

2. Dry coffee grounds for fertilizer between paper towel for a few minutes. So good for your plants.

3. Place fresh meat from the market in the microwave for 10 seconds at 100% power. This extends the freshness in the refrigerator by 3 or 4 days.

4. Make lots of pancakes and freeze the left overs. When ready to use warm each portion for 20 - 30 seconds or until hot at 100% power. Serve with syrup which has also been heated in the microwave.

5. Heating milk or whipping cream prolongs the life of the product. Two minutes at 100% power for each cup. Cool and refrigerate.

6. Refresh dried brown sugar by placing one slice of bread in container with sugar. Cover and cook 30 - 45 seconds at 100% power to soften.

7. Freshen day old rolls and cookies for a few seconds at 100% power. Be sure not to overcook.

8. Try sprinkling meats with brown gravy mix or bottled browning for a great brown flavor. Don't add salt as it toughens. (Try the various types of Micro-Shake if they sell it in your area. You are in for a treat if you do.)

9. Dry older bread for croutons. Microwave 4 cups for 5 - 7 minutes at 100% power.

10. Small amounts of food and sauces come out of jars and containers more easily if heated 10 - 20 seconds at 100% power. Saves lots of food!!

11. Freshen chips and crackers 1 minute (2 cups) at 100% power, uncovered.

12. For low calorie cooking use a tablespoon of water or boullion juice instead of butter. Replace milk/butter/flour sauce with broth/cornstarch mixture.

13. Easy removal of nut shells is accomplished by placing 2 cups of nuts and 1 cup of water in covered glass casserole and heating for 1 - 2 minutes at 100% power.

14. Rewarm homemade cookies for a few seconds for that "just baked" flavor.

15. Heat ice cream container in microwave for a few seconds to make it easier to scoop. Also, place a scoop of ice cream on "yesterday's pie" and heat for 10 - 15 seconds. The pie will be warm and the ice cream will not be melted.

16. Toast coconut by spreading ½ cup of coconut into a pie plate and cook, uncovered, 3 - 4 minutes at 100% power until golden ... stir once or twice during cooking.

17. When freezing a casserole which is to be heated or cooked by probe, insert a straw into the middle of the casserole where the probe is to be inserted. Freeze the food in the bowl in which you plan to cook it. After it is frozen, "pop" it out of the container, wrap it for the freezer with cooking directions written plainly on the package. When ready to cook, simply unwrap, slip it back into the proper bowl. If the probe is being used, remove the straw and place the probe in its place. Defrost and cook according to directions. If no probe is being used, follow directions above except leaving out the straw and cooking by time only.

18. A roast may be frozen, defrosted and cooked by probe later if you insert a straw in the spot you plan to place the probe. When ready to cook, remove straw and insert probe. Roast is now ready to defrost and cook.

19. Warm finger towels by placing four small towels in a non-metallic basket after you have wet them and heat in microwave for 1 - 2 minutes at 100% power. This is especially nice to offer your guests before or after dinner if

you use a drop of vanilla, almond, etc., in the water before heating. Gives such a nice scent.

20. Warm Compress can be made by heating a wet wash cloth for 15 - 30 seconds at 100% power.

21. Hot Compress may be made by heating a wet wash cloth for 30 - 45 seconds at 100% power.

22. For softening tortillas, place four to six tortillas between dampened paper towels and microwave at 100% power for 20 - 40 seconds. This saves not only the time that it takes when you soften them in grease or oil on top of the stove, but it also saves the calories.

23. Warm cheeses, which have been in the refrigerator, to serving temperature by placing in the microwave and heating for 15 - 45 seconds (according to denseness of cheese) at 30% power.

24. You may "proof" bread dough in the microwave by placing the dough in a buttered loaf pan, covering with wax paper and microwaving for 3 - 4 minutes at 10% power. Let stand for 10 - 15 minutes and repeat until dough has doubled in size.

TABLE OF CONTENTS

Appetizers 1

Eggs, Cheese, Grain and Pasta 9

Soups, Salads and Sandwiches 31

Fruits and Vegetables 41

Entrees 55

Desserts and Sweets 91

Potpourri 117

Table of Contents

Appetizers

Eggs • Cheese • Grain and Pasta

Soups • Salads and Sandwiches

Fruits and Vegetables

Entrées

Desserts and Sweets

Potpourri

notes:

DID YOU KNOW?

Perk one tablespoon powdered dishwashing detergent and a full pot of water to get your coffee pot really clean.

A thimble over the percolator stem before you measure in the coffee will prevent it from getting clogged ... Be sure to remove before perking!

If a dish is cracked, boil it for 45 minutes in sweet milk and the crack will "weld" together. It will be hardly visible and will be strong enough to stand the same usage as before.

For a quick counter cleanup (vegetable peels, crumbs, etc.) whisk them into a dust pan that has been stuck under the counter edge.

To get a car out of the mud, snow, or sand, let a little of the air out of the tires and drive off.

Freshen a lunch box by leaving a piece of bread dampened with vinegar on the inside.

Keep a toothbrush by the kitchen sink as it is great for cleaning beaters, graters and other kitchen utensils.

Salting water hastens boiling process.

Whiten shoe laces by washing them in sour milk.

So that syrup bottle caps will loosen easily, give the top of the bottle a "spritz" of no-stick vegetable oil.

Uncovered liquids release moisture, causing refrigerator to work overtime; therefore costing you more to run. Keep them covered!

Store ice cubes in a brown bag and they won't stick together.

Before emptying your vacuum cleaner bag, sprinkle a newspaper with water and when emptied onto the paper there will be no scattering of dust.

Take a vinyl tablecloth instead of a blanket for picnics. Spread vinyl side down to keep out ground moisture.

A pinch of salt in your coffee grounds before brewing intensifies and improves the flavor.

Dip a new broom in hot salt water before using as it toughens the bristles and makes the broom last longer.

Tool caddy for gardening can be made from an old golf bag. It has places for tools, towel, etc. ... even has wheels!

Clean barbecue grate easily by placing cool grate inside a large plastic garbage bag with ½ cup powdered dishwasher detergent and enough hot water to cover the grill. Seal, shake and let stand several hours and then rinse thoroughly.

Wax your ashtrays and the odors won't linger nor will the ashes cling. Saves washing as they can be wiped clean with a paper towel.

APPETIZERS

ARTICHOKE DIP

2 (14 oz.) cans artichoke hearts, drained and finely chopped

8 oz. Parmesan cheese, grated
1 pint mayonnaise

Mix chopped artichokes with cheese and mayonnaise in two quart container. Microwave at 100% power for 5 - 8 minutes, uncovered, stirring once, until mixture is bubbly and hot. Serve with crackers.

BROCCOLI CHEESE DIP

1 can cream of mushroom soup
16 oz. processed cheese, cubed
8 oz. cream cheese
1 pint sour cream
1 (10 oz.) pkg. frozen broccoli, chopped

3 stalks celery, chopped
1 (4 oz.) can mushrooms, chopped
1 can water chestnuts, chopped
1 med. onion, chopped
Dash of red pepper sauce

Place package of broccoli on saucer and cook in package (poke several holes for draining) on 30% power for 4 minutes. Drain well and set aside. Saute onion, celery, mushrooms and water chestnuts in large measuring cup (or in casserole before adding cheese, etc.) at 100% power for about 4 minutes or until onions are transparent. Combine sauteed vegetables with broccoli, cheese, sour cream, soup and seasoning and cook covered at 50% power for about 9 - 10 minutes or until piping hot. Serve with chips, crackers or fresh vegetables. To be so healthy, this is almost everyone's favorite and it makes a sensational sauce on vegetables.

CHILI CON QUESO

½ c. onion, chopped
1 Tbsp. butter
2 med. sized tomatoes, peeled and chopped (16 oz. whole tomatoes may be substituted for fresh)

5 - 7 dashes hot pepper sauce
1 tsp. garlic
1 lb. processed cheese, cubed
1 - 2 hot chili peppers, seeded and chopped

Melt butter in 1½ qt. container about 45 sec. at 100% power. Add chopped onions, tomatoes, peppers, along with seasonings, saute 1 - 3 min. at 100% power, uncovered, until onion is transparent or cooked. Add cheese, cover, cook 5 - 8 min. 50% power until cheese is well melted. Stir well, serve with tortilla chips

CHILI DIP

8 oz. cream cheese
½ c. sliced green onions
4 oz. chopped green chilies

16 oz. can chili without beans
1½ c. grated Cheddar cheese

Soften cream cheese and spread over bottom of 9 inch pie plate. Sprinkle with green onions, chilies and spread chili over the top of cream cheese and vegetable mixture. Top with grated Cheddar cheese and microwave at 70% power, * covered, 2 - 5 minutes until bubbly hot. Serve with chips.

* I've reduced the heat when cooking this cheesy delight so the cheese won't "string" which can sometimes happen with hot heat.

CHIMALE DIP

1 (15 oz.) can tamales
1 (15 oz.) can chili con carne
¼ c. picante sauce (mild to hot, according to taste)

8 oz. processed cheese, cut into cubes
¼ c. grated cheese

Drain tamales, remove wrappers and mash with fork in dish you plan to cook and serve in. Combine mashed tamales, chili, picante sauce and cheese. Heat at about 100% power, uncovered, 10 - 15 minutes until hot and bubbly. Sprinkle with grated cheese. Serve with corn chips or tortilla chips. This is truly a favorite whenever I serve it ... everyone tries to guess that "special" ingredient ... the tamales.

MEXICO CITY DIP

1 lb. lean ground beef
1 Tbsp. browning/seasoning powder, optional
1 can (16 oz.) refried beans
1 can (4 oz.) diced green chiles, undrained
1 jar (8 oz.) taco sauce (desired hotness)

1 c. (4 oz.) shredded Cheddar cheese
1 c. (4 oz.) shredded Swiss or Monterey Jack cheese
10 pitted ripe olives, sliced

Cook beef in cook/drain cooker* after sprinkling with browning for 4 - 5 min. at 100% power, uncovered. Stir or break meat into small pieces. In 9 inch dish layer beans, beef, chiles and taco sauce. Cover with waxed paper and cook at 70% power for 8 - 10 minutes until heated through. Top with cheese and olives and cook, uncovered, for additional 3 - 5 minutes until cheese melts. Let stand a couple of minutes before serving. *Use a colander in a pie plate if you don't have a cook/drain cooker.

HOT CLAM DIP

2 (6½ oz.) cans minced clams
   (drain and reserve ¼ c.
   liquid)

12 oz. cream cheese, softened
½ c. butter, softened
Dash of garlic powder

Place clams and ¼ c. clam liquid in a 1 qt. container, covered. Microwave for 5 minutes at 100% power. Stir butter and cream cheese into clams and cook for 1 ½ - 2 minutes at 100% power. Stir until smooth and serve hot with crackers. I have been able to use a hot heat on this quick recipe as I only heat until it is "warm," not really cooked. If it were a dish requiring extended time in the cooking, I would have to lower the temperature as dairy and cheese products tend to break down and string requiring lower temperature to prevent this.

PIZZA FONDUE

1 onion, chopped
½ lb. lean ground beef
2 Tbsp. margarine, optional
2 (10½ oz.) cans pizza sauce
1 Tbsp. cornstarch

1½ tsp. oregano
½ tsp. basil
¼ tsp. garlic powder
10 oz. grated Cheddar cheese
1 c. grated Mozzarella cheese

Place meat and onion in drain and cook container with margarine (optional)* and cook for 3 - 4 minutes at 100% power, uncovered. Mix cornstarch and seasonings with pizza sauce and mix with meat mixture. Stir well. Cook additional 2 - 5 minutes until mixture thickens and is bubbly. Add cheese gradually, cooking at 50% power a minute at a time until cheese is melted. Serve this with garlic bread cubes or toasted English muffin cubes. *You only need to add butter as a flavoring, like vanilla. It will be absorbed during the standing time when added then and it isn't needed when you saute in microwave cooking like in conventional cooking. Therefore, you have this option.

Sour cream may be frozen and then processed in blender. It will gain a thinner, but smooth consistency.

MEXICAN CHICKEN

Chicken drummettes or breasts
   (bite size) 2½ - 3 lbs.
1 pkg. (1½ oz.) taco seasoning
   mix

1 c. bread crumbs, finely
   chopped

Mix crumbs and seasoning. Coat chicken and place in circle fashion* on roasting rack or layers of paper towel, a few (6 - 8) pieces at a time. Cook, covered with paper towel for 6 minutes per pound at 100% power. Allow to

3

stand a few minutes, uncovered after cooking before serving. * This recipe calls for arranging food in a circle with nothing in the center of the plate. Just remember that this lets food receive microwaves from both sides as well as top and bottom all at the same time. It saves time in rearranging and causes much more even cooking.

CHICKEN LIVER RUMAKI

1 lb. chicken livers, cut in half*
1 (8 oz.) can whole water chestnuts, drained and cut in half*

Bacon slices, cut in thirds or halves
Teriyaki sauce

Marinate water chestnuts for several hours in sauce. Wrap bacon pieces around a piece of liver and a piece of water chestnut and secure with toothpick. Place about six at a time in circle fashion on rack. Baste with sauce, cook covered with a paper towel for 3 - 5 minutes at 100% power until bacon is crisp. (Rumaki will take 6 minutes per pound to cook.) *You may also use dates stuffed with cream cheese for a change, but pre-cook bacon for a couple of minutes and shorten cooking time slightly for cooking date/bacon combination. (Sweet and Sour Sauce may also be used in this recipe if desired.) Allow Rumaki to stand a few minutes before serving to allow them to finish cooking. These may all be cooked and then put in chafing dish for serving if desired.

VEGETABLE RUMAKI

1 bag (16 oz.) frozen broccoli, cauliflower and carrot mixture
¼ c. catsup
¼ c. soy sauce

1 clove garlic, minced
2 Tbsp. cider vinegar
1 lb. bacon, thinly sliced
2 Tbsp. brown sugar

Combine vegetables, catsup, soy sauce and garlic in 1½ qt. casserole. Cover and microwave at 100% power for 2½ - 3½ minutes or until partially thawed. Mix in vinegar and set aside. Cut bacon slices in half all at once and place one half of section on rack and cover with paper towel. Microwave at 100% power for about 4 minutes. Separate slices and cook additional 1 - 2 minutes, pliable but partially cooked. Repeat with remaining bacon. Let cool until bacon is cool enough to handle. Assemble by placing a piece or two of vegetables at each end of bacon strips. Roll and secure with toothpick. Place 6 - 8 pieces at a time in circle fashion on rack. Sprinkle with brown sugar, cover with paper towel and cook 4 - 7 minutes at 100% power until bacon crisp. Repeat. Serve hot. Try these marinated vegetables sometime by themselves as a salad or relish ... DELISH!

FRANK KABOBS

8 frankfurter pieces (2
    frankfurters)
8 olives
8 pineapple chunks

4 tsp. oil
2 tsp. soy sauce
2 tsp. pineapple juice
2 tsp. brown sugar

Put a piece of each ingredient on toothpick, making a total of eight ka-bobs from this recipe. Combine sauce ingredients. Place kabobs circle fashion on rack and brush each with sauce. Cook 1½ - 2 minutes at 100% power. Turn over and baste. Cook an additional 2 minutes at 100% power. Serve immediately.

MEATBALLS DELUXE

2 lbs. ground beef
1 egg, slightly beaten
1 large onion, grated
1 can water chestnuts, chopped
1 c. bread crumbs, optional

Salt to taste
1 bottle chili sauce
Juice from 1 lemon
½ med. sized jar of grape jelly

Combine beef, egg, onion, salt, water chestnuts and bread crumbs, mixing well. Form into small individual meatballs. Place meatballs in circle fashion on plate or rack. Combine chili sauce, lemon and jelly and baste meatballs. Cook meatballs 5 - 6 minutes per pound at 100% power. (May cover with paper towel to prevent splattering.) Let meat stand to finish cooking and continue with rest of meatballs. Serve with extra sauce.

MEATBALLS AND SWEET/SOUR SAUCE

Meatballs:

1 lb. ground beef
1 Tbsp. finely chopped onion
1 Tbsp. finely chopped parsley
¼ c. water chestnuts, chopped,
    opt.
½ c. soft bread crumbs

1 egg, slightly beaten
2 Tbsp. milk
1 tsp. salt
¼ tsp. garlic salt
⅛ tsp. allspice
⅛ tsp. cloves

Sauce:

1 c. unsweetened pineapple
    juice
2 Tbsp. brown sugar

1 Tbsp. cornstarch
1 Tbsp. lemon juice

Sauce: Combine pineapple juice, brown sugar and cornstarch in 2 cup measure. Cook uncovered for about 2 minutes at 100% power until thickened, stirring once. Add lemon juice and set aside.

Meatballs: Combine beef, onion, parsley, crumbs, egg, milk and spices. Form into approximately 40 balls (about 1 inch in diameter). Place 8 balls in a circle on rack or on paper plate lined with paper towel.* Baste with sauce, cover with waxed paper and cook for 1½ minutes at 100% power. Continue with remaining meatballs. Serve remaining sauce in small container for dipping. *As I have said before, arranging in circles, with a hole left in the center will let microwaves enter food from all sides for even cooking.

MUSHROOMS IN GARLIC BUTTER

½ c. butter or margarine
1 Tbsp. finely chopped green
   onion tops
3 garlic cloves, minced

2 Tbsp. finely chopped parsley
Dash of seasoned pepper
1 lb. fresh mushrooms

Blend butter, onion, garlic, parsley and pepper. Cover and chill. (This will keep in refrigerator if it is all not used.) Clean mushrooms*, removing stems (reserve these and use in another recipe). Fill each cap with ¼ tsp. of butter and arrange in circle fashion in round serving dish. Cook 1 - 2 dozen mushrooms, uncovered at 100% power for 2 - 4 minutes. Rotate dish once. *When you clean mushrooms, don't soak in water. They are like a sponge and will soak up the dirt. Therefore, clean with a damp cloth or brush off dirt with small brush so mushrooms won't get a "dirty" taste.

STUFFED MUSHROOMS

32 fresh mushrooms, med. sized
1 pkg. (10 oz.) frozen chopped
   broccoli
½ c. soft bread crumbs, finely
   chopped
2 Tbsp. chili sauce
2 Tbsp. lemon juice

1 tsp. salt
⅛ tsp. pepper
1 Tbsp. chopped parsley
2 Tbsp. butter
⅓ c. onion, minced
Parmesan cheese, grated

Clean mushrooms, remove and chop stems. Pierce broccoli package with fork and place in bowl or on plate in microwave oven. Cook at 50% power to defrost for 4 - 5 minutes. Drain and cook additional 2 - 3 minutes, drain again. Combine drained broccoli, chopped mushroom stems, bread crumbs, chili, lemon, salt, pepper and parsley. Cook butter and onion in 2 cup measure uncovered for 3 minutes at 100% power. Add butter and onion to broccoli mixture. Stuff mushroom caps generously. Place 8 mushrooms in circle on paper plate lined with paper towels. Sprinkle with cheese, cover with waxed paper and cook each full plate for 2 minutes at 100% power. I have covered these with a waxed paper lid so a bit of steaming will occur. Remember, waxed paper is your "crack the lid" cover in microwave cooking or in other words, when you want some steam to stay in and some to escape.

GARLIC SHRIMP

1½ lb. shrimp, peeled and
   deveined
4 whole garlic cloves, peeled
5 Tbsp. olive oil

1 Tbsp. lemon juice
½ tsp. tarragon
Dash red pepper sauce
Hot Lemon Butter (see recipe)

Place prepared shrimp in a ring mold; add garlic, oil, lemon juice and spice. Microwave for 4½ - 6 minutes at 100% power, uncovered, until shrimp are pink. Allow to stand a few minutes and serve hot with Hot Lemon Butter. 10 - 12 servings.

Don't forget ... shellfish is cooked only 3 minutes per lb., if cooked alone. You will have to extend this recipe time a fraction, however, to compensate for the liquid that has been added.

TORTILLAS IN CHILI SAUCE

1 med. onion, sliced in rings
1 Tbsp. cooking oil
1 (10 oz.) can of tomatoes and
   green chilies, chopped with
   liquid
1 (14½ oz.) can tomatoes,
   drained and chopped
1½ tsp. salt

12 corn tortillas, cut in ½ inch
   wide strips
6 - 8 oz. Monterey Jack cheese,
   grated
4 jalapeno peppers (green
   chilies for milder flavor),
   seeded and chopped

Place onion and oil in 8x12 inch baking dish covered with plastic wrap and microwave at 100% power for 4 - 5 minutes until tender. Add tomatoes and salt. Place tortilla strips in tomato mixture and toss, coating well. Cover again with plastic wrap and microwave for 3 minutes at 100% power, stirring once. Add cheese and peppers on top of mixture and again cover with plastic wrap and microwave additional 2 minutes at 100% power. Cut in small squares to serve.

SHRIMP APPETIZER TREE

½ - 1 lb. shrimp, cooked and
   deveined
1 bunch leaf lettuce
1 bunch radishes or other
   favorite vegetables

1 piece Cheddar cheese, ¾ x 4 x
   4 inch
Florist picks
Styrofoam cone
Toothpicks

If shrimp is not cooked place shrimp on glass plate in circle fashion or in ring mold.* Sprinkle with herbs and microwave at 100% power for 3 minutes per pound. Cool shrimp, peel and devein. Take radishes and other vegetables and decorate (see garnish chart). Place in cold water. Cube cheese.

Place Styrofoam cone on Styrofoam circle, securing with florist picks or on plate, secured with tape. Take lettuce and starting at the base of cone, attach, stem side up, securing with picks as you go. Layer up to top with remaining leaves to resemble green tree foliage. In ornament fashion place shrimp, vegetables and cheese, securing with long toothpicks, to resemble decorated Christmas tree. Place tree on serving plate and serve as appetizers. *Remember when arranging this shrimp on plate, or in ring mold to make it cook more evenly, you should not have it over 1 to 1½ inches in depth as microwaves only penetrate about ¾ - 1 inch into the food. Therefore, keep the layer thin so when cooking in circle arrangement microwaves can go in each side of arrangement as well as up and down, giving one way cooking to all food without stirring.

HOT HERBED PRETZELS

2 Tbsp. butter
½ tsp. tarragon
2 tsp. parsley

¼ tsp. salt
¼ tsp. onion powder
2 c. pretzels

Place butter in 2 quart container for 30 - 40 seconds at 100% power. Blend in seasonings, add pretzels and toss. Heat for 1½ minutes at 100% power until heated through, stirring once.

notes:

Eggs • Cheese • Grain and Pasta

DID YOU KNOW?

Eggs peel more easily if a teaspoon of salt is added while boiling. Plunge immediately into ice water for 10-15 minutes. Gently roll eggs to "shatter" the peeling. They will scoot right off.

To seal eggs when they crack during boiling, add a little vinegar to the water.

A teaspoon of salt in the water prevents the eggs from cracking during boiling.

How fresh are your eggs? In a bowl of cool water:

1. A very fresh egg will sink and lie horizontally on bottom. (High yolk and compact white.)

2. A week old egg will lie tilted up. (White will be more liquid.)

3. Two to three week old egg will stand upright. (Yolk will spread out ... watery white will run.)

4. Four week or older, egg will float and should be thrown out.

Wet knife to keep egg yolks from crumbling when slicing hard-cooked eggs.

Bread crumbs added to scrambled eggs will improve the flavor and also will make larger helpings.

A touch of vinegar in water when poaching eggs help to set the whites so they will not spread.

EGGS, CHEESE, GRAIN AND PASTA

EGGS - CHEESE

BAKED EGGS

1 egg   **1 tsp. milk**

Grease 6 oz. custard cup. Break egg into bowl and top with milk. Cover with plastic wrap and cook for ¾ - 1 minute per egg at 50% power. Let stand 1 - 2 minutes covered before serving.

FRIED EGGS

1 - 6 eggs   **¼ tsp. butter per egg**

Preheat browning skillet for 3 - 5 minutes (according to number of eggs being cooked) at 100% power. Dot with butter and add eggs. Cook as follows:

      1 egg - 30 to 45 seconds at 100% power
      2 eggs - 45 seconds to 1 min. at 100% power
      4 eggs - 1 to 1¼ min. at 100% power
      6 eggs - 1¼ to 1¾ min. at 100% power

If your browning dish has a lid, cover to cook. If, after cooking time is done, let stand to finish cooking or, if you wish "over easy" the eggs. Let them stand a few seconds, then serve. You may also cook eggs for ⅔ of the time, then turn and cook the remaining ⅓ of the time. This will give you a more solid yolk. DO NOT OVERCOOK EGGS. Try this a few times and you will be an old hand at egg cookery.

"MICROWAVE" HARD-BOILED EGGS

Use 1 - 6 eggs. Grease 6 oz. custard cup or small ring mold, according to the number of eggs being cooked. Crack eggs and place liquid eggs into proper container. Pierce each egg several times. Cover with plastic wrap and cook at 50% power for 1 - 1½ min. per egg (shorter time required for multiple eggs). Let stand and cool before slicing or chopping. This is an excellent way to prepare eggs for salad, etc. so you won't ever have to peel an egg again.

POACHED EGGS

1 egg   **2 Tbsp. water**
¼ tsp. vinegar

Place water and vinegar in small custard cup and bring to boil (30 - 45 seconds at 100% power). Place egg in boiling water. Cover with plastic wrap. Reduce heat to 50% power and cook for 45 sec. to 1½ min. (desired doneness varies according to personal taste). Swirl dish and let stand covered for 1 - 2 minutes before serving. You may cook several eggs at once following these directions, but using a bit larger bowl.

SCRAMBLED EGGS

Eggs
Water or milk

Seasonings
Butter, optional

Mix desired number of eggs with ½ - 1 tsp. water or milk per egg. Add desired seasonings, except for salt. Cook ½ - ¾ min. per egg (degrees of desired doneness vary) at 100% power. For large quantities of eggs you may wish to lower temperature for the last half of cooking time. Stir eggs several times during cooking. Let eggs stand to finish cooking. (Eggs will not look cooked until standing.) Salt and butter added at last.

BREAKFAST ON A BUN

1 tsp. butter
1 egg, beaten
1 slice Canadian bacon, ham or bologna

1 slice (¾ oz.) processed cheese
Round bun, toasted, if desired

Place butter in glass pie plate. Microwave at 100% power for 30 seconds; add egg. Cover with waxed paper, microwave for 45 - 60 seconds, at 100% power until set. Fold egg into quarters, top with meat and cheese. Microwave for 15 seconds or until cheese is melted at 100% power. Place in bun. Makes one serving.

EGGS BENEDICT

English muffin, split, buttered and toasted
1 egg

3" square of ham or Canadian bacon
Paprika

Mock Hollandaise Sauce:

2 Tbsp. butter
1 c. mayonnaise

2 - 4 Tbsp. lemon juice

Follow directions in this book for poached eggs. While eggs are standing combine the butter in 2 cup measure and heat at 100% power for 30 - 45 seconds. Stir in mayonnaise and lemon juice. Heat for 2 - 3 minutes at 50% power until just hot. DO NOT BOIL. Next, warm ham (2 slices) 45 seconds at

100% power. Cover with towel to keep warm. Combine the Eggs Benedict by placing warmed ham or bacon on buttered muffin, top with egg and hot Hollandaise. Sprinkle with paprika, if desired. Heat 45 seconds - 1 minute per egg at 50% power.

FRAMED EGG

1 slice toast, buttered   **1 egg**

Cut 3 inch circle in toast and place on plate. Break egg into hole and cover with plastic wrap. Cook for 30 - 45 seconds at 100% power to desired doneness. Let stand and season.

SPECIAL SCRAMBLED EGGS

1 Tbsp. butter (optional)
½ c. onion, chopped
¼ c. green pepper, chopped
**   (optional)**
5 slices bacon, cooked and
**   crumbled**

4 eggs
1 c. evaporated milk
⅓ tsp. hot sauce
½ tsp. salt
⅛ tsp. pepper
¾ c. Cheddar cheese, shredded

Place onion and green pepper in 9" pie plate, along with butter. Microwave covered at 100% power for 1 - 2 minutes. Sprinkle vegetables with bacon pieces and let stand. Beat eggs and milk with spices. Pour egg mixture over bacon and vegetables. Cover with wax paper and microwave for 1 - 2 minutes at 100% power. Stir slightly and continue to microwave for 3 - 6 additional minutes at 50% power, stirring several times. Sprinkle with cheese and microwave at 50% power for 1 - 2 minutes until cheese is melted. Let stand covered for 1 minute before serving.

Mixed eggs may be frozen for several months for use later.

EGGS DELISH

½ c. milk
1 (3 oz.) pkg. cream cheese
6 eggs
1 c. ham, diced
1 large tomato, cut in wedges
**   (optional)**

½ green pepper, diced (optional)
½ tsp. salt
¼ tsp. pepper
Dash Worcestershire sauce
Dash Tabasco, optional
2 Tbsp. butter, optional

Heat milk in 1 cup measure for 45 seconds - 1 minute at 70 - 100% power until milk is warmed. In larger container soften cheese for 30 seconds at 100% power and beat until fluffy. Mix in milk and eggs. Stir in ham. Place butter in 10 inch glass pie plate and melt for 30 - 45 seconds. Add green pepper and cook, covered for 45 seconds at 100% power. Add green pepper and tomato wedges to egg mixture. Place in pie plate and cook, covered for 8 - 10 minutes at 50% power, stirring several times. Allow to stand a couple of minutes for eggs to firm as they will appear slightly soft after cooking.

BASIC OMELET

1 Tbsp. butter
3 eggs
3 Tbsp. milk

Dash salt and pepper
⅔ c. favorite filling*

Prepare filling for omelet and set aside. Place butter in 9" pie plate and microwave for 30 - 45 seconds at 100% power until melted. Beat eggs, milk and spices. Add to pie plate. Cover tightly with plastic wrap. Microwave 70% power for 1½ minutes. Gently lift edges and allow uncooked eggs to flow underneath. Cover completely with plastic wrap and microwave an additional 1 ¼ - 1¾ min. until set. Let stand covered for 1 minute. Fill, fold and serve immediately. *You may use vegetables, cheese, meat, etc. as filling ... let your imagination run wild.

DUTCH OMELET

1 small onion, chopped
½ green pepper, chopped
2 c. potatoes, shredded
½ lb. ground sausage
¾ tsp. salt, divided

6 eggs
½ c. milk
⅛ tsp. pepper
Dash of cayenne

Cook sausage and onion for 3 - 5 minutes at 100% power. Drain well. Place drained sausage aside and add ½ tsp. salt. Combine eggs, ½ tsp. salt, milk, pepper and cayenne. Place 1 Tbsp. sausage grease and potatoes in round casserole and pour egg mixture over this. Sprinkle with sausage and microwave uncovered for 3 minutes at 100% power. Lift edges of omelet with spatula to distribute eggs, but do not disturb potatoes. Reduce heat for 6 - 7 minutes to 50% power. Rotate if cooking is uneven. Remove when almost set and tent for 2 minutes.

MEXICAN OMELET ROLL

1 strip ham (1½ inches wide and
    6 inches long)
¼ c. margarine or butter,
    optional
½ c. green pepper, chopped

1 med. onion, chopped
5 eggs, beaten
¼ c. water
2 Tbsp. pimento, chopped

Cheese Sauce:

1 can Cheddar cheese soup
½ c. milk
½ tsp. seasoning salt

Dash Worcestershire sauce and
Tabasco

Place meat in baking dish, covered, and microwave for 3 - 4 minutes at 70% power until warmed through. Cover with aluminum foil and allow to stand while cooking eggs. Add butter, if desired, along with green pepper and onion in 8 x 12" baking dish. Cover and cook 3 - 4 min. at 100% power until vegetables are tender. Stir together eggs and water and pour over vegetables. Sprinkle with pimento. Cover with plastic wrap and microwave until set, but still glossy, for 8 - 10 minutes at 100% power. Turn dish when necessary for even cooking. Remove plastic wrap and loosen bottom and edges of omelet with spatula. Cover dish with plastic wrap and invert onto cookie sheet. Place ham on small end of eggs and roll, jelly roll fashion. Place seam side down on serving dish. Top with sauce if desired. Four servings.

Sauce should be combined and cooked for 3 - 4 minutes at 100% power.

FARM COUNTRY EGGS

4 slices bacon
2 Tbsp. butter
6 oz. frozen hash brown
   potatoes
¼ c. chopped onion
¼ c. chopped green pepper
6 eggs

¼ c. milk
½ tsp. salt
¼ tsp. basil, optional
Dash of pepper
1 c. (4 oz.) Cheddar cheese,
   shredded

Place bacon on rack, cover with paper towel and cook for 4 minutes at 100% power or until done. Cool, crumble and set aside. Place butter, potatoes and vegetables in an 8" round dish, such as a cake plate. Cook uncovered for 6 minutes at 100% power, stirring once. While vegetables are cooking mix eggs, milk and seasonings. Flatten potato mixture and pour the eggs over the top. Cover with plastic wrap and microwave at 70% power for 5 - 7 minutes or until the eggs are almost set. Stir once. Sprinkle bacon and cheese over top. Heat uncovered for additional one minute until cheese starts to melt. Remove and let stand for 5 minutes before serving.

BACON AND CHEESE CASSEROLE

4 slices of bacon
1 c. milk
2 c. Swiss or Cheddar cheese,
   grated
½ c. canned onion rings

¼ c. green chilies, optional
¼ c. green onions, diced
Pepper
Basil
3 eggs

Cook bacon for 3 - 5 minutes at 100% power until crisp. Set aside until cool and crumble. Beat together eggs and milk; add cheese and remaining ingredients. Pour into 8 inch pie plate. Cook, uncovered for 6 - 8 minutes at 100% power (lower temperature to 70% power and cook for 8 - 12 minutes if you have time ... product quality will be better). Stir once during cooking time and let stand 6 - 10 minutes or until set in middle. Makes 4 servings.

ENCHILADAS MONTEREY

2 large onions, chopped
2 green chilies, seeded and
  chopped
2 c. sour cream
2 cans (10 oz.) red enchilada
  sauce

1 dozen corn tortillas
1 lb. Monterey Jack cheese, cut
  into strips
2 c. Cheddar cheese, shredded
Salt to taste

Place onion in 8 cup measure and microwave for 1½ - 2 minutes at 100% power. Add chilies and salt, place in another container and set aside. In 8 cup measure blend sour cream and enchilada sauce. Heat at 50 - 70% power until bubbly. Dip tortillas, one at a time in sauce to soften.* Place in 12 x 8" baking dish, one tortilla at a time, spooning a part of onion mixture in center, topping with Jack cheese and rolling. Place seam side down in pan and repeat until all tortillas are filled. Top with remaining sauce and sprinkle with Cheddar cheese. Cover with wax paper and microwave 70% power about 1½ minutes per enchiladas until very hot.

*Tortillas may be softened by wrapping in a dampened towel and microwaving for 30 - 45 seconds on 100% power if time is short and you wish to hurry the above procedure.

QUICHE DELUXE

1 (10 inch) pie shell, baked
5 - 6 slices bacon, cooked and
  crumbled
5 eggs
1 c. sour cream
1 tsp. seasoning salt
¼ tsp. pepper

1 med. onion, sliced
1 med. green pepper, cut into ¼
  inch strips
4 oz. fresh mushrooms, sliced
2 Tbsp. butter, optional
1 Tbsp. flour

Put crumbled bacon into cooked pie shell and set aside. Mix eggs, cream and seasonings. Set aside. In a 1 quart measure saute onion, green pepper and mushrooms (use butter here if desired) for 3 - 5 minutes, uncovered, at 100% power. Add flour and mix well. Add to the egg mixture and stir until blended. Pour into pie crust and microwave for 12 - 14 minutes at 70% power or until metal knife inserted in center comes out clean. Foil ring may be used for shielding ... (a circle with no center) ... so that the center will get the same amount of microwave energy as the rest of pie. See charts and utensil section of this book for more explanation.

QUICHE WITH HASH BROWN POTATO CRUST

24 oz. pkg. frozen hash brown
    potatoes, thawed
¼ c. butter, melted
¼ tsp. each of paprika and
    Worcestershire sauce
1 c. (4 oz.) shredded jalapeno
    pepper cheese

1 c. (4 oz.) shredded Gouda
    cheese
8 oz. diced shredded ham
⅓ c. cream or evaporated milk
    (generous)
2 eggs, beaten

Place potatoes in dish, blot well with paper towel to absorb moisture. Push up on sides of dish to form pie crust. Brush with butter combined with paprika and Worcestershire sauce. Place potatoes in microwave and cook uncovered for about 4 - 5 minutes at 100% power. While crust is baking mix remaining ingredients except for eggs. Place filling in potato shell and pour beaten eggs over this for topping. Bake at 70% power for 7 - 10 minutes, uncovered until filling is set. Let stand for 5 - 10 minutes before serving.

BROCCOLI-RICE QUICHE

2 c. cooked Minute rice
4 - 5 oz. Cheddar cheese, grated
3 eggs
1 tsp. salt
1 pkg. (10 oz.) frozen chopped
    broccoli

½ c. chopped onion
½ tsp. seasoning salt
¼ tsp. garlic powder
½ tsp. pepper
1 Tbsp. milk
1 small can mushrooms

Combine rice, ¾ cup cheese, 2 eggs, slightly beaten and ½ tsp. salt. Press into greased dish to resemble pie shell. Set aside. Defrost broccoli* for 4 minutes at 50% power. Drain and mix with onion in bowl. Microwave at 100% power for 6 minutes, covered. Let stand for 3 minutes and beat in remaining egg. Stir in seasonings, milk and mushrooms. Mix well and spoon into rice shell. Cook 8 - 10 minutes at 60% power and sprinkle with remaining cheese after cooking. Microwave another 20 seconds or so for cheese to melt. Let stand a minute or two before serving.

*I always defrost my vegetables and drain before cooking them so they will be more crisp, like fresh, instead of soggy. This can happen if cooked and defrosted at the same time like most cookbooks suggest.

SAUSAGE STRATA

1 lb. ground pork sausage
8 slices bread, cubed
2 c. grated Cheddar cheese
4 eggs
2 c. milk
1 Tbsp. chopped chives

1 Tbsp. chopped green pepper
(optional)
½ tsp. dry mustard
½ c. crushed French fried
onions, optional

In cook/drain container microwave sausage* at 100% power for 5 - 6 minutes until no longer pink. In greased 12 x 8 inch baking dish, place alternate layers of bread cubes, sausage and cheese, starting and ending with bread cubes. Beat together eggs, milk and spices. Pour over bread cubes and cover in refrigerator for at least 4 hours and preferably overnight. Sprinkle with crushed onion rings and microwave uncovered at 70% power for 14 - 18 minutes or until knife comes out clean when inserted near center. Let stand a few minutes before serving.

*Add chives and green pepper at this stage.

BREADS

GARLIC BREAD

1 loaf French, Italian or
　　sourdough bread
½ c. (1 stick) butter or
　　margarine, melted

2 garlic cloves, minced
½ c. grated Parmesan cheese
Paprika

Cut loaf into slices 1 inch thick without cutting all the way through to bottom. Set loaf on microwave safe rack or in paper napkin-lined basket.

Combine butter and garlic and blend well. Using pastry brush, coat slices of bread with garlic butter. Sprinkle with cheese and paprika. Cook on high or 100% power until heated through, 1 to 2 minutes.

PULL APART BACON BREAD

2 cans buttermilk biscuits
1 c. chopped green pepper
1 c. chopped chives

½ lb. bacon (8 slices)
½ c. Parmesan cheese
½ c. margarine, melted

Cook bacon and crumble. In 2 cup measure cook vegetables at 100% power, covered, for 1 - 2 minutes until tender; drain well. Mix vegetables and bacon. Cut biscuits into fourths and dip each piece in butter, cheese and vegetable/bacon mixture. Arrange uncovered in two small ring pans or 1 large ring pan. Cook at 50% power for 4 - 7 minutes for small pan and 10 - 15 minutes for large. Do not overcook. Bread will finish cooking during the standing time.

SAVORY CHEESE BREAD

2 c. flour
1 Tbsp. dry onion flakes
2 tsp. poppy seed
1½ tsp. baking powder
½ tsp. salt

½ c. shredded Cheddar cheese
¼ c. plus 2 Tbsp. butter
⅔ c. buttermilk or sour milk
1 egg, slightly beaten
2 tsp. sugar

Topping:

1 tsp. butter
2 Tbsp. grated Parmesan
　　cheese

1 tsp. poppy seed
Dry onion soup mix, optional

Combine flour, onion, etc. Cut in butter like pastry. Add milk and egg. Turn into 10 inch pie plate that has been lightly greased. Sprinkle with topping and make several ½ inch deep criss-cross cuts. Cook uncovered 6 - 9 minutes, turning once if necessary, at 70% power. Let stand 10 minutes. Serve in wedges.

SWEET CHERRY NUT BREAD

1 c. cooking oil	1 tsp. baking powder
1½ c. sugar	1 tsp. soda
4 eggs	1½ tsp. salt
1 can (15¼ oz.) crushed	1 c. bing cherries, chopped
pineapple, undrained	1 c. nuts, chopped
1 tsp. almond flavoring	1 to 2 Tbsp. graham cracker
3½ c. all purpose flour, unsifted	crumbs

Blend oil and sugar in 8 cup measure and add eggs one at a time, beating well after each addition. Stir in the pineapple and flavoring and add remaining ingredients except crumbs. Stir until well mixed. Grease two 8 x 4" or 9 x 5" loaf dishes or use large ring mold. Sprinkle with crumbs and pour in batter. Microwave (one loaf at a time) uncovered for 10 minutes at 50% power and then 3 minutes at 100% power until surface is no longer doughy. Cool bread 10 minutes and turn out. Cool completely and then wrap tightly and store in refrigerator for at least 3 or 4 hours before slicing. If wrapped tightly you may freeze for up to 3 months. Remember, if ring mold is used baking time must be lengthened. Also, you only cook one layer of a full cake or bread recipe at a time, never both unless cooked in a ring mold.

SOUR CREAM COFFEECAKE

Cake:

¾ c. sugar	1¼ c. flour
⅓ c. cooking oil	½ tsp. salt
2 eggs	½ tsp. soda
¾ c. sour cream	½ tsp. nutmeg
½ tsp. vanilla	

Glaze:

2 Tbsp. butter	¼ tsp. maple flavoring

Topping:

2 Tbsp. butter	½ - ¾ tsp. cinnamon
⅓ c. brown sugar, packed	⅓ c. pecans, chopped
3 Tbsp. flour	

Blend sugar and oil. Beat in the eggs one at a time and then stir in sour cream and vanilla. Add dry ingredients and beat until smooth. Grease bottom of 8 inch glass dish and pour half of batter into this. Set aside. In a small cup or bowl place butter and microwave at 100% power for 10 - 15 seconds until softened. Mix in brown sugar, flour, cinnamon and nuts until crumbly. Spoon half of topping evenly over batter in dish. Spoon remaining batter over topping evenly. Sprinkle with remaining topping. Microwave at 70% power uncovered for 6 - 7½ minutes, rotating if necessary. Cook additional 1½ - 2 minutes on high if needed until top is no longer doughy. Let stand 5 minutes. Microwave butter for glaze at 100% power for 20 - 40 seconds until melted. Blend in maple flavoring and brush glaze over surface of cake. Serve warm. Remember when you cook baked goods in your microwave they cook much more evenly if you will elevate the pan slightly by setting it on an inverted saucer or a rack if you have one so that the microwaves don't get trapped underneath.

MEXICAN CORN BREAD

½ lb. bacon, cooked and
　crumbled
¾ c. yellow corn meal
1 egg
¾ c. buttermilk
¾ tsp. baking soda
¾ tsp. salt
1 tsp. garlic powder
¼ c. bacon fat (reserved from
　bacon)

1 small can green chilies,
　optional
1 (8¾ oz.) can cream style corn
1 c. onion
1 jalapeno pepper, seeded and
　chopped, optional
1½ c. grated mild Cheddar
　cheese

Place bacon grease in 8 cup measure along with corn meal, egg, buttermilk, soda, salt and garlic powder. Stir in onion, chilies, cheese and bacon. Pour into a greased 9 inch round dish and microwave for 11 - 13 minutes at 70% power. Rotate for even cooking if necessary. Slice and serve warm.

UPSIDE DOWN BRUNCH CAKE

3 Tbsp. margarine
⅓ c. brown sugar
1 (9 oz.) pkg. corn bread mix

6 pineapple rings
6 slices Canadian bacon

Place butter and brown sugar in 9 inch round cake pan and microwave for 1 min. at 100% power. Stir and cook an additional minute so syrup will caramelize. Prepare the cornbread batter according to package directions and set aside. In bottom of cake pan, on syrup, place one pineapple ring in the center and remaining rings around it. Place a piece of bacon on top of each pineapple ring and top with cornbread batter. Cook cake for 8 - 12 minutes at 70% power. Let cool several minutes and turn onto serving plate. Cut into wedges and serve with hot maple syrup.

MUFFINS ALL GONE

1½ c. flour	½ c. soured whipping cream*
⅓ c. sugar	¼ c. milk
½ tsp. baking powder	3 Tbsp. cooking oil
½ tsp. soda	1 egg
½ tsp. salt	¼ c. nuts, chopped
¼ tsp. nutmeg	1 Tbsp. sugar
½ tsp. allspice	½ tsp. cinnamon

Combine flour, sugar, baking powder, soda, salt and spice. Mix well. Combine cream, milk, oil and egg. Beat well. Add this to the flour mixture and mix until smooth. Spoon mixture into 12 paper muffin cups filled ⅔ full and sprinkle with nuts. Combine 1 Tbsp. sugar and cinnamon and mix well. Sprinkle this on the muffins. Microwave in circle fashion, six muffins at a time, uncovered for 1¾ - 2¼ min. at 100% power. Serve warm or cool.

*Excellent way to use whipping cream which has gotten old.

CARAMEL NUT ROLL

2 - 3 Tbsp. butter	¼ c. maraschino cherries,
½ c. brown sugar	halved or quartered
2 Tbsp. corn syrup	1 roll (10 oz.) canned refrigerator
½ c. pecan halves	biscuits

Melt butter in 8" round dish for 30 seconds at 100% power. Mix in ½ brown sugar and syrup. Place a glass, open end up in the center of dish to form a ring mold.* Place nuts and cherries in syrup. Arrange biscuits, cut in halves and rolled in remainder of brown sugar, on top of nuts and cherries. Microwave for 3 - 5 minutes at 50% power, uncovered, being careful not to overcook. Cool slightly and turn onto plate, leaving dish inverted for a while so glaze will run.

*I have made a ring mold by using a glass so microwave will cook from all sides (in/out/up/down). If this isn't done the center will have only two way cooking (up/down) and nut roll won't cook evenly.

GRAINS AND PASTA

CHEESE GRITS

½ c. grits
2 c. water
1 tsp. chicken bouillon granules
¼ - ⅓ c. butter or margarine
Dash of garlic salt

1 egg, well beaten
4 oz. garlic or jalapena cheese,
    cubed
1 small can chopped green
    chilies, drained (optional)

Bring water *and chicken granules* to a boil in a 2 quart casserole, covered, approximately 4-5 minutes at 100% power. Add grits, cover with waxed paper, and microwave 3 minutes at 100% power. Add butter, green chilies and slowly stir in egg. Add cheese and garlic salt. Stir until melted. (Grits may be made to this point early in the day and cooked later.) Microwave, uncovered, at 50% power for 7-8 minutes or until bubbly, turning if necessary for even cooking. If browning is desired, lower heat to 25-30% power and slow cook until edges brown and center is firm.

Remember, if doubling this recipe that you will need to add approximately double the cooking times.

GREEN RICE

3 c. cooked rice
1 (10 oz.) pkg. frozen spinach,
    thawed and drained
¾ c. finely chopped green
    onions with tops
½ c. grated Cheddar cheese
½ c. chopped fresh parsley
    (may substitute ¼ c.
    dehydrated)

½ c. slivered almonds
¼ c. chopped green pepper
¼ c. margarine
2 tsp. lemon juice
1 tsp. seasoning salt
1 clove garlic, minced
1 egg, beaten
1 c. milk
Paprika, optional

Mix rice, spinach, onions, cheese, parsley, almonds, peppers and garlic in 2 quart casserole. Blend the rest of the ingredients and mix with the rice mixture. Let this stand in the refrigerator until thoroughly cooled so the flavors will blend. Sprinkle with paprika if desired and cook for 18 - 20 minutes at 70 - 80% power until it is like custard. Let stand for 5 - 10 minutes before serving. This is a recipe you don't cover since you want the top to be slightly crusty ... same as you would want it if cooked conventionally ... therefore, similar methods must be used, such as no cover and medium hot heat!

HERBED RICE

1 c. water
1 c. Minute rice
1 cube/tsp. chicken bouillon
1 tsp. parsley

½ tsp. basil
¼ tsp. thyme
Touch garlic powder, optional

Bring water to boil, approximately 2 minutes at 100% power, uncovered. Add spices and rice. Cover tightly with plastic wrap and allow to stand for 5 - 6 minutes.

MACARONI AND CHEESE

1 - 1½ c. uncooked macaroni
2 Tbsp. flour
¼ c. chopped onion
1 tsp. salt
Dash pepper
½ tsp. dry mustard
Dash Tabasco or hot sauce

1 c. milk
1 c. water
2 Tbsp. butter
1 - 1½ c. (4 or 5 oz.) cubed
   Cheddar cheese
Bread crumbs, optional

In 3 quart casserole combine macaroni, flour, onion, seasonings. Stir in liquid and dot with butter. Cook covered tightly for 10 - 12 minutes at 100% power until macaroni is about tender, stirring once or twice. Blend in cheese, sprinkle with crumbs and let stand for 3 - 5 minutes until cheese is melted through.

NOODLE PUDDING

1 (10 oz.) pkg. med. noodles
4 eggs
½ c. sugar
1 (12 oz.) carton sour cream
1 (12 oz.) carton creamed
   cottage cheese

Salt to taste
½ c. fine crumbs
2 - 3 Tbsp. butter, melted
Paprika

Melt butter for 30 - 45 seconds at 100% power and stir into bread crumbs. Set aside. Cook and drain noodles according to package directions or microwave directions in this book. Beat the eggs, sugar, sour cream, cottage cheese and salt together until blended. Add noodles and pour into an 8 x 12 inch dish or equivalent round dish. Of course the round dish is better as the cooking will be much more even. (If you don't understand the reason for this look for more explanation under utensil chart in this book.) Sprinkle with buttered crumbs and paprika and cook at 50% power for 15 - 25 minutes, uncovered, until hot and set. (Lower temperature used because of dairy products ... don't forget.)

VEGETABLE FETTUCCINI

16 oz. fettuccini noodles*
5 green onions, sliced
2 garlic cloves, minced
6 c. broccoli, uniform pieces
½ tsp. salt - optional
1¼ tsp. basil
½ tsp. oregano

2 tomatoes, cut into wedges
1 zucchini or 1 c. frozen peas,
   optional
1 c. grated Parmesan cheese
8 Tbsp. whipping cream
4 Tbsp. butter

According to instructions in this book, cook the noodles in the micro-wave or conventionally as directed. Drain and rinse in cold water, set aside. Combine vegetables, seasonings except salt in 2 qt. casserole and cook, cov-ered, for 4 ½ - 6 minutes at 100% power. If not cooked in ring mold, stir once. Combine vegetable mixture with cheese, cream and salt. Toss well with noo-dles. Add the butter, cover and microwave for 3 - 6 minutes at 100% power until heated through, stirring once. Serve after a few seconds. *(If you wish, save half of mixture by putting in freezer. Will freeze for up to 6 months. Then cook only ½ of noodles and use only ½ of cheese, cream and butter to combine the other half of mixture for use. Also, if cooking only half, shorten cooking time to 1½ - 3 minutes at 100% power.)

PASTA PRIMAVERA

3 Tbsp. olive oil
1 clove garlic
1 med. onion, chopped
1 small green pepper, chopped
½ tsp. basil
1 tsp. parsley
¼ - ½ crushed red pepper
½ tsp. oregano
Salt and pepper to taste
1 c. each of 3 or 4 of following:
   Asparagus, zucchini,

   mushrooms, cauliflower,
   broccoli, carrot, etc. (cut
   into uniform pieces)
1 large tomato, chopped in large
   pieces
½ c. heavy cream
½ c. chicken broth
¾ - 1 c. grated Parmesan cheese
8 oz. spaghetti, cooked

Combine olive oil, garlic, spices, except for salt, onion and pepper. Stir fry (uncovered) for 1 - 2 minutes at 100% power until vegetables partially soft. Add vegetables, except tomato and cook for 5 - 10 minutes, stirring occasion-ally, until vegetables start to become tender. Add tomato, cook 1 minute more at 100% power.* Add liquid and simmer, 70% power until vegetables are ten-der. Add spaghetti and cheese, tossing lightly. Serve immediately.* Add salt if desired.

Notice how similar Microwave method for stir-frying is to conventional stir-frying.

MEXICAN LASAGNA

¼ c. chopped green pepper
½ c. chopped onion
2 Tbsp. butter or margarine
1 can (4 oz.) diced green chilies, drained
3 eggs
1 c. small curd creamed cottage cheese
½ tsp. salt
½ tsp. oregano
¼ tsp. ground cumin
⅛ tsp. pepper
4 c. broken tortilla chips, divided
2 c. shredded Monterey Jack cheese, divided
2 c. shredded Cheddar cheese, divided
1 c. sour cream

Combine onion, green pepper and butter. Uncovered, cook for 1½ - 2 minutes at 100% power. Stir in green chilies and set aside. Mix together eggs, cottage cheese and seasonings. Sprinkle 1½ c. chips over bottom of 12 x 8" dish. Spoon half of cottage cheese mixture over chips. Spread half of onion mixture over cottage cheese and sprinkle with 1½ c. Monterey Jack cheese and 1 c. Cheddar cheese. Repeat chips, cottage cheese and onion layers. Microwave for 5 minutes uncovered, at 100% power and then reduce power to 50% for 9 - 14 minutes or until center is firm. Rotate once, if cooking is uneven. Combine remaining cheese and sour cream. Spread over casserole and sprinkle with remaining chips. Microwave for 3 - 5 minutes, uncovered, at 100% power until sour cream mixture is heated. Let stand a minute or two before serving. (100% power can be used in this last procedure because we heat only - not actually cook; otherwise, dairy products take lower heat.)

ONE STEP LASAGNE

1 lb. ground beef
2 jars (15½ oz.) meatless spaghetti sauce
½ c. water
1 tsp. salt
1 (8 oz.) pkg. uncooked lasagne noodles
2 c. Ricotta cheese, drained
3 c. shredded Mozzarella cheese
½ c. grated Parmesan cheese
Parmesan cheese (optional)
Parsley
1 egg

Using cook/drain container, cook ground beef for 4 - 5 minutes at 100% power. Salt, add water and sauce to beef. Mix egg and Ricotta. In 9 x 13" dish, (or two smaller dishes) spread ⅓ sauce. Cover with ½ of noodles, half of cheese mixture and sprinkle with 1 cup Mozzarella. Repeat once and top with remaining meat sauce. Sprinkle with ½ cup of Parmesan cheese. Cover tightly with double thickness of plastic wrap. Cook for 30 minutes at 50% power. Uncover, sprinkle with remaining Mozzarella and additional Parmesan. Cook, uncovered at 50% power for 2 minutes or until cheese is melted. Allow to stand for a few minutes, sprinkle with parsley and serve. Remember if using two small dishes cook only one at a time, but for ½ the time.

GREEN NOODLES WITH RICH MEAT SAUCE

½ c. diced onion
½ c. diced carrot
½ c. diced celery
1 lb. ground beef
¾ c. dry white wine
⅓ - ½ c. milk
1 can (35 oz.) plum tomatoes,
   chopped

½ Tbsp. tomato paste
1¾ tsp. salt
⅛ tsp. nutmeg
⅛ tsp. pepper
½ c. heavy cream
5 Tbsp. chopped fresh parsley
1 - 1½ lb. green spinach noodles

Cook noodles according to microwave directions or directions on package. In cook/drain container, cook vegetables and ground beef for 4 - 6 minutes at 100% power. In 4 qt. casserole place beef mixture and remaining ingredients, except for cream. Simmer at 50% power until thick and bubbly (10 - 15 min.). Stir in heavy cream, heat until very hot. Place sauce over noodles and sprinkle with fresh parsley.

EASIER THAN LASAGNE CASSEROLE

8 oz. narrow egg noodles
1 lb. ground beef
1 small onion, chopped
1 clove garlic, minced
1 can (6 oz.) tomato paste
½ tsp. salt

½ tsp. chili powder
⅛ tsp. pepper
½ c. water
4 oz. cream cheese
1 c. cottage cheese

Cook and drain noodles as directed and set aside. In cook/drain dish brown ground beef, onion and garlic for 4 - 6 minutes at 100% power until no longer pink, stirring once. Place ground beef mixture in bowl or 8 cup measure. Stir in tomato paste, salt, chili powder, pepper and water and set aside. Microwave the cream cheese in a 1½ qt. glass casserole for 20 - 30 seconds at 100% power. Blend until smooth and mix with cottage cheese. To the cheese mixture add the noodles and spread evenly in dish. Top with meat mixture, cover and microwave for 9 - 11 minutes at 100% power until heated through. Let stand about 10 minutes before serving.

BEEF TETRAZZINI

2 lbs. ground beef
½ c. chopped onion
1 tsp. salt
½ tsp. pepper
1 pkg. (10 oz.) frozen broccoli,
   thawed*

1 pkg. (8 oz.) spaghetti or
   linguini
¼ c. (2 oz.) shredded Swiss
   cheese

Cheese Sauce:

½ c. margarine
¼ c. flour
½ tsp. salt

2 c. (8 oz.) shredded Swiss
  cheese
2¾ c. milk

Prepare spaghetti as directed on package. Place ground beef and onion in cook/drain container and cook at 100% power for 6 - 8 minutes until beef is almost cooked, stirring to break up, if necessary. Add broccoli*, stir in salt and pepper and set aside. In 8 cup measure melt butter for about 2 minutes until melted. Stir in ¼ c. flour and salt, blending well. Gradually add milk and cook at 100% power for about 4 minutes until slightly thickened, stirring occasionally. Stir in 2 cups shredded cheese and allow to melt. Combine beef/vegetable mixture and Cheese Sauce with spaghetti. Spoon into 9 x 13" baking dish or two 9" baking dishes. Bake, covered with plastic wrap for 8 - 20 minutes at 50% power until very hot. Uncover, sprinkle with ¼ c. shredded cheese and bake another 1 - 1½ min. at 50% until cheese is melted. Allow to stand for a few minutes before serving.

*Fresh broccoli or zucchini which has been partially cooked can be used when in season. Also cook less time for small pan and one pan at a time.

CHART FOR COOKING CEREAL:

Item	Container	Amount of Water	Cereal	Salt	Time
Oatmeal (Old Fashioned)	1 quart	¾ cup	⅓ cup	Dash	3 - 5 min.
Oatmeal (Quick)	16 oz.	¾ cup	⅓ cup	Dash	1 - 2 min.
Cream of Wheat	1 quart	1 cup	2½ Tbsp.	Dash	3 - 4 min.
Cream of Wheat (Instant)	per pkg.	per pkg.	per pkg.	Dash	½ - 1 min.

Mix cereal with hottest tap water. You will notice large bowls are used in proportion to amounts of cereal. This prevents boil over. Cook at 100% power, uncovered and stir half-way through the cooking time. Tip: You might like to add a dip of ice cream instead of cream and sugar sometime.

CHART FOR COOKING RICE AND OTHER GRAINS:

Item	Container	Amount of Hot Water	Approx. Time To Boil Water 100% Power	Cook Time 30% Power	Stand Time
Brown Rice 1 cup	2 qt. bowl	3 cups	5 - 6 min.	40 - 50 min.	15 min.
Mixed Rice (6 oz.)	2 qt. bowl	2 c. or per pkg. direct.	4 -5 min.	20 - 25 min.	5 - 10 min.
Long Grain Rice- 1 c.	2 qt. bowl	2 cups	4 - 5 min.	14 - 16 min.	10 min.
Quick Rice 1 cup	1 qt. bowl	1 cup	2 - 3 min.	5 min.	5 min.
Short Grain Rice - 1 c.	2 qt. bowl	2 cup	4 - 5 min.	10 - 12 min.	10 min.
Instant Rice 1 cup	2 qt. bowl	1 cup	2 - 3 min.	1 min. (optional)	5 - 10 min.
Grits ⅔ cup	3 qt. bowl	3½ c.	5 - 6 min.	10 min.	10 min.

Always cook rice, covered well. Also, larger amounts should be stirred once to separate the grains before the long cooking time takes place. You may add bouillon cubes and desired spices to water before boiling, if you wish. You will also notice that cooking rice and grains in the microwave does not save time, but it will give you a good product.

CHART FOR COOKING PASTA

Item	Container	Amount of Hot Water	Approx. Time To Boil Water	Cook Time 50% Power	Stand Time
Egg Noodles (8 oz.)	3 quart	1½ qts.	8 - 10 min.	10 - 11 min.	3 min.
Elbow Macaroni (8 oz.)	3 quart	1½ qts.	8 - 10 min.	12 - 14 min.	3 min.
Lasagna* (8 oz.)	Bake Dish 12" x 8"	1½ qts.	8 - 10 min.	18 - 19 min.	3 min.
Spaghetti (8 oz.)	3 quart	1½ qts.	8 - 10 min.	12 - 14 min.	3 min.
Specialty (shells, bows, etc.)	3 quart	1½ qts.	8 - 10 min.	15 - 17 min.	3 min.

When cooking pasta you should add 1 tsp. of salt and ½ Tbsp. of cooking oil to the water. Also, coat the rim of the container with cooking oil (this helps prevent boil over). After water comes to a boil, add pasta. * With the exception of Lasagna and then you will find that if you bring water to boil in another container and pour over the lasagna, you will have better results. Cook for the recommended time, uncovered, stirring a couple of times. Slightly undercook pasta that will be reheated or cooked in a casserole as otherwise it may become too soft. After testing for doneness allow to stand for the recommended minutes and then drain and rinse before using.

Write Your Recipes Here:

notes:

Soups • Salads and Sandwiches

DID YOU KNOW?

Rinse slightly wilted lettuce briefly with hot water and place it in refrigerator to freshen.

Peel oranges, grapefruits, and tree fruits entirely from membranes or white pulp under skin by soaking fruit 5 minutes prior to peeling.

Fruit, tomatoes, and avocadoes ripen best in a brown paper bag.

For a tearless way to chop onions refrigerate or soak in cold water before chopping. A snorkel mask may also be worn for very "teary" onions.

Onions will be milder in taste if soaked in milk for an hour or two, then drained. Better yet ... microwave each onion for 30 seconds to one minute at 100% power (according to size). They will become much less strong, but will still have the "crunch" of a raw onion ... no heartburn either.

Use bottom half of green pepper first as the top half will remain fresher.

Store lemon and limes in a tightly closed container and they will keep for weeks.

One teaspoon of vinegar added to any gelatin recipe will keep molded salads and desserts from melting away easily.

Place garlic bud in cabinet or cutting board and press the side of bud with knife blade. Peeling will come right off.

Sprinkle orange, lemon, lime or pineapple juice on fruits to keep them from turning dark.

Prevent salads from becoming soggy and wilty by drying greens, draining canned foods and using just enough dressing to moisten. Always add dressing at last minute for raw vegetables.

Use pickle juice for the following:

1. Whisk a bit of oil and a tablespoon of mustard or use plain for salad dressing.
2. Heat to boiling point and pour over shredded cabbage for a wonderful slaw.
3. Blend into mayonnaise, yogurt or sour cream for a pourable dressing.
4. Use as a marinade.
5. Season tomato based gelatine salads, tomato based drinks or soups.
6. Use as part of the liquid in lemon and lime jello.

SOUPS, SALADS AND SANDWICHES

SOUPS

CREAM OF BROCCOLI SOUP

1 large bunch broccoli
⅓ c. onion, chopped
2 c. water
4 chicken bouillon cubes
1 garlic clove, minced
½ tsp. thyme
2 Tbsp. butter

3 Tbsp. flour
¼ tsp. white pepper
1½ c. light cream or half & half
¼ c. sour cream
2 Tbsp. chopped chives,
  optional

Cut broccoli into uniform pieces. Place in large casserole with onion. Cover with plastic wrap and cook for 6 minutes per pound until vegetables are tender. If not cooked in ring mold, vegetables may have to be stirred for even cooking. Make bouillon from cubes and water and add this with garlic and thyme to vegetable mixture. Puree until smooth. Set pureed mixture aside and melt butter in 4 cup measure. Stir in flour. To this mixture add pepper and gradually add cream, stirring well. Cook at 70% power for 3 - 5 minutes, stirring occasionally until thickened (may cook 2 - 3 minutes at 100% if necessary). Blend in broccoli puree and heat through. Ladle into bowls. Top with dollop of sour cream and sprinkle with chives. You will notice I lower the temperature once the cream is added. If time allows, you should always do this when dealing with dairy products.

QUICK AND EASY CLAM CHOWDER

½ c. minced onion
¼ c. diced celery
1 Tbsp. butter, optional
3 slices bacon, fried crisp and
  crumbled
1 can (10¾ oz.) cream of potato
  soup

1 can (10¾ oz.) cream of celery
  soup
¼ tsp. thyme
¼ tsp. nutmeg
⅛ tsp. pepper
1 - 2 cans minced clams, drained
1 pint half & half

Place vegetables in 8 cup measure, cook for 1 min. at 100% power. (Cook uncovered if butter is used, cover with plastic wrap if not.) Stir in soups, spices and clams. Gradually stir in the cream and blend until smooth. Heat for 10 - 18 minutes at 50 - 70% power until piping hot. Add bacon and serve immediately.

OLIVE CARROT CREAM SOUP

1 lb. carrots, pared, sliced	1 c. stuffed green olives
1 c. chopped onion	¼ tsp. grated lemon peel
1 can (13¾ oz.) chicken broth	⅛ tsp. pepper
1 c. water	1 c. light cream

In 8 cup measure or ring mold place carrots and onion. Cover with plastic wrap and cook for 6 - 7 minutes at 100% power until vegetables are tender after standing. Add broth and water. Pour into electric blender and blend until smooth. Stir olive mixture into soup. Add a bit more water if thinner soup is desired. Chill overnight. Serve garnished with slices of olives and carrots.

MEXICAN CHEESE SOUP

1 med. tomato, peeled and chopped	1 can cream of potato soup
2 cans (4 oz.) green chilies, seeded, rinsed, cut in strips	1 can cream of onion soup
	1 can evaporated milk
½ tsp. garlic salt	2½ c. water
¼ tsp. pepper	2 c. (8 oz.) Monterey Jack cheese, cubed

In 8 cup measure combine tomatoes, chilies, garlic salt and pepper. Microwave for 1 - 1½ minutes at 100% power. Blend in liquids. Heat at 50% power for 12 - 18 minutes or until hot. Divide cheese into serving bowls and pour hot soup over cheese. Serve at once.

TORTILLA SOUP

1 small onion, chopped	1½ c. tomato juice
1 can (4 oz.) green chilies, chopped	1 tsp. ground cumin
	1 tsp. chili powder
2 garlic cloves, crushed	1 tsp. salt
1 c. tomatoes, peeled, chopped	⅛ tsp. pepper
1 can (10¾ oz.) condensed chicken broth	2 tsp. Worcestershire sauce
	1 Tbsp. bottled steak sauce
1 can (10½ oz.) beef broth	3 tortillas, cut in ½ inch strips
1⅓ c. water	¼ c. shredded Cheddar cheese

In 8 cup measure cook onion, chilies and garlic, covered, at 100% power for 1 - 1½ minutes or until onion is soft. Add tomatoes, broths, water, tomato juice, spices and sauces. Bring soup to boil, uncovered, at 100% power, approximately 8 - 10 minutes. Reduce heat to 50% - cover and simmer for approximately 15 minutes. Add tortilla strips and cheese and simmer an additional 2 - 3 minutes.

SALADS

GOURMET ASPARAGUS SALAD

1 pkg. (10 oz.) frozen asparagus
   or substitute fresh when in
   season
1 can (15 oz.) artichoke hearts,
   drained and halved
⅓ c. olive oil or salad oil

¼ c. lemon juice
1 clove garlic, halved
½ tsp. salt
4 lettuce cups
¼ c. sliced ripe olives
Fresh ground pepper

Cook fresh asparagus for approximately 6 minutes per pound, covered, at 100% power or for frozen, defrost and drain and then cook covered for 4 minutes. In bowl combine drained and cooked asparagus with artichoke hearts. Sprinkle with freshly ground pepper. Combine oil, lemon, garlic and salt. Pour over vegetables. Cover and chill for several hours, tossing once or twice. Drain and remove garlic. Arrange vegetables in lettuce cups; top with olive slices and serve.

AVOCADO SALAD WITH GRAPEFRUIT AND BACON

½ c. diced bacon (2 - 3 oz.)
1 pink grapefruit, peeled or
   canned grapefruit sections,
   drained
1 ripe avocado, cut lengthwise
   into 12 pieces
½ c. grapefruit juice
¼ tsp. salt

1 tsp. olive oil
1 tsp. sugar
¼ tsp. ground pepper
2 Tbsp. finely chopped red
   onion
Parsley or watercress (garnish),
   optional

Place bacon on rack and cook according to instructions in book for bacon until medium crisp. Drain and pat dry, discarding fat. Peel grapefruit, removing outside membrane and white pith if using fresh. Divide sections. Toss the avocado in the grapefruit juice to coat. Remove and reserve juice. On two warm plates arrange alternating slices of avocado and grapefruit sections. Sprinkle with salt. In 2 cup measure combine bacon with olive oil and cook, at 100% power, until bacon is quite crisp. Add sugar, pepper and juice. Cook for 30 seconds at 100% power until warmed through. Pour bacon dressing over salads and sprinkle with onion. Garnish if desired.

GAZPACHO SALAD

1 c. chopped tomato
½ c. chopped cucumber
¼ c. chopped green pepper
2 Tbsp. sliced green onion
½ c. bottled French dressing

1 tsp. lime juice
½ tsp. oregano
⅛ tsp. cracked black pepper
2 avocado halves, peeled
1 qt. iceberg lettuce, shredded

Combine tomato, cucumber, green pepper, green onion, dressing, lime juice and seasoning. *Mix lightly. Fill avocado halves with vegetable mixture. Serve on shredded lettuce. 4 servings. *Heat dressing, lime juice, spices for one minute at 100% power. This helps the flavors to blend better ... then add your vegetables.

GOLD DOLLAR SALAD

2 lbs. carrots, scraped, sliced
1 can tomato soup
¾ c. sugar
¼ c. vinegar
1 tsp. salt

¼ tsp. prepared mustard
½ c. salad oil
3 small onions, in rings
1 green pepper, diced (optional)
1 c. frozen green peas (optional)

Cook carrots, covered in a ring mold for about 12 minutes, or 6 minutes a pound at 100% power. Remember to cook these in a ring mold so you'll get the even "4 way cooking" and you won't have to stir like you would if cooking without the cone in the center. If you don't have a ring mold, take a regular casserole and set a glass upright in the center. Make your own. Mix all other ingredients and add carrots. Marinate for at least 24 hours. Serve hot or cold. This is a dish that will keep for 10 days to two weeks.

SPINACH SALAD

1 large bowl spinach
⅛ lb. bean sprouts
12 bacon strips, fried and
    crumbled (per directions
    this book)
3 - 4 hard boiled eggs, chopped
    (per directions this book)

¼ lb. mushrooms, sliced
⅓ red onion, cut into rings
1 can water chestnuts, finely
    chopped

Dressing:

1 c. vegetable oil
½ c. white sugar
⅓ c. brown sugar

½ c. wine vinegar
1 Tbsp. Worcestershire sauce
1 med. onion, finely grated

Following the directions set out in this book, cook bacon, six strips at a time, on rack, cover with paper towel. Mix dressing and allow to stand for flavors to blend, preferably several hours. Mix eggs slightly in ring mold and cook according to directions for hard cooked eggs in this book. Allow to cool and then chop. Combine salad and dressing. Serve immediately. This serves a large group, but recipe may be halved if desired.

SPINACH SALAD WONDERFUL

2 Tbsp. sherry wine vinegar
2 egg yolks
2 tsp. Dijon mustard
1 tsp. fresh or ½ tsp. dried
　tarragon
¼ tsp. salt
Freshly ground pepper
2 c. oil

2 lbs. spinach, stems discarded
　(washed and dried)
3 c. shredded Swiss cheese
¾ lb. fresh mushrooms, sliced
½ lb. bacon, crisply cooked,
　drained and chopped
3 eggs, hard cooked, chopped
Tomato wedges (garnish)

Combine first six ingredients and blend with whisk. Slowly add oil, whisking constantly. Store in tightly covered container (may be stored for one week). Place spinach in large bowl. Add cheese, mushrooms, bacon* and eggs*. Toss with just enough dressing to coat lightly. Garnish with tomatoes. Serve with additional dressing. (*Follow directions in this book for cooking bacon and hard cooked eggs.)

DIVINE VEGETABLE SALAD

1 large head cauliflower, cut into
　flowerets
1 bunch broccoli, cut into
　flowerets
½ lb. fresh mushrooms, sliced
1 c. diced celery
½ c. chopped onion
4 oz. artichoke hearts, halved
1 can (4 - 6 oz.) black olives,
　drained

1 - 1½ c. cherry tomatoes,
　halved
1 bottle Italian dressing
1 c. mayonnaise
¾ Tbsp. chili sauce
2 Tbsp. lemon juice
2 tsp. dill weed
1 tsp. salt

Heat Italian dressing for 1 - 2 minutes at 100% power and pour over all vegetables and marinate overnight or longer. Combine mayonnaise, chili sauce, lemon, dill and salt. Drain vegetables and top with mayonnaise sauce. Let stand several hours before serving.

PRETZEL SALAD

1½ c. crushed pretzels
½ c. sugar
⅓ c. oleo
1 pkg. (9 oz.) frozen whipped
　topping
8 oz. cream cheese

½ c. confectioners sugar
2 pkgs. (3 oz.) strawberry gelatin
1 pkg. (16 oz.) frozen
　strawberries, undrained
1 c. crushed pineapple, drained

Melt oleo at 100% power for 30 - 45 seconds and combine with sugar and pretzels. Place in 9 x 13" pan and microwave uncovered at 70 - 80% power for 2 - 4 minutes. Set aside and let cool. Mix cream cheese, topping and powdered sugar and spread over crust. Place in refrigerator to partially set. In 8 cup container heat 2 cups water and add gelatin. Heat additional minute or two at 100% power until gelatin is completely dissolved. Add strawberries and pineapple and refrigerate until partially set. Pour on top of other two layers and refrigerate until very firm.

SHERBET SALAD

1 pkg. (3 oz.) Jello (lime, lemon
  or orange)
1 pint sherbet (pineapple, lime
  or orange)

1 small can pineapple tidbits
1 small bottle maraschino
  cherries (red)

Bring one cup of water to boil, about 2 minutes in microwave at 100% power. Stir in Jello and cook additional 30 - 40 seconds at 100% power. Stir until Jello completely dissolves. Blend in sherbet (this mixture will be frothy). Drain juice from pineapple and cherries, add to mixture and mold in 9 inch square pan or ring mold. Chill 4 - 5 hours.

PASTA-SALMON SALAD

1 can (7¾ oz.) salmon
1 c. uncooked small sea shell
  macaroni*
¼ c. bottled Italian dressing
½ c. diagonally sliced celery
¼ c. chopped green onion
3 Tbsp. chopped parsley
½ tsp. grated lemon peel
⅛ tsp. dried dill weed

Dash pepper
½ c. mayonnaise
½ tsp. cream-style horseradish
Lettuce
Tomato slices and cucumber
  slices
Radishes and green peas,
  optional

Drain salmon, reserving 1 Tbsp. liquid. Break into large chunks. Cook and drain macaroni; toss with Italian dressing and chill. Combine pasta, salmon, celery, green onion, cucumber, peas, parsley, lemon, dill and pepper. Chill thoroughly. Combine mayonnaise and horseradish. Line bowl with lettuce, then with slices of tomato and cucumber. Spoon salad in center and garnish with radishes and peas. Serve with mayonnaise mixture (4 - 5 servings). *May cook macaroni in microwave per directions in book.

RICE SALAD

4 c. cooked rice
¼ c. Italian salad dressing
½ c. diced green pepper
2 green chilies, chopped
½ c. chopped green onion
½ c. chopped celery
½ c. sweet pickle relish,
    optional
2 hard cooked eggs, chopped
⅓ c. sliced ripe olives, optional

⅓ c. bean sprouts, optional
2 c. shredded fresh spinach,
    optional
¼ - ½ tsp. nutmeg
½ - 1 Tbsp. curry powder
1 - 2 tsp. mustard
1 Tbsp. soy sauce, optional
½ tsp. sugar
⅓ c. mayonnaise

Cook rice according to microwave directions if desired. Mix rice with Italian dressing and set aside to cool. Mix sauce and remaining vegetable ingredients you wish to use. Cool completely before serving.

CHICKEN SALAD

3 c. diced and cooked chicken
1½ c. chopped celery
2 Tbsp. chopped parsley
1 tsp. salt
½ tsp. pepper

½ c. heavy cream, whipped
1 c. mayonnaise
2 Tbsp. lemon juice
½ c. slivered almonds, toasted

Cook chicken on rack in circle fashion, meatiest portions to outside for 6 minutes per lb. at 100% power. Cool. Dice chicken and combine with celery, parsley, salt and pepper in large bowl. Mix well. Gently fold in whipped cream, mayonnaise, lemon juice and almonds, combining well. Refrigerate for at least 1 hour before serving.

CHICKEN SALAD A LA ORANGE

1 chicken breast, skinned and
    boned
2 Tbsp. sliced almonds
2 Tbsp. salad dressing
1 tsp. lemon juice
½ tsp. honey

Dash of salt
⅓ tsp. curry powder
½ c. green seedless grapes
1 or 2 oranges
¼ c. coconut, optional

Cook chicken breasts on meat rack*, covered, for 6 minutes per pound. Cool. Microwave almonds in small dish, uncovered, for 2 - 2½ minutes at 100% power, stirring occasionally until lightly toasted.

Cube chicken and mix with salad dressing, lemon, honey and seasonings. Mix in grapes and chill. Slice off a thin layer from one end of each orange and cut almost through orange to form 8 wedges. Place orange on serving plate, separating each wedge to coconut. *Don't forget to arrange the chicken in a circle arrangement. You won't have to rearrange if you "think circles", leaving the middle vacant for even cooking. If you do have something cooking in the middle, that piece may have to be rearranged and moved to the outside where more cooking is taking place. (Outside of pan cooks up, down and in: Middle of pan cooks up and down only. See chart in this book on cooking patterns.)

PINEAPPLE FILLED WITH FRUITED CHICKEN

1 breast of chicken, boned and
   skinned
½ c. shredded coconut
½ c. sliced almonds or cashews,
   toasted
1 can (11 oz.) mandarin orange
   sections, drained
½ c. sweet orange marmalade

¼ c. teriyaki sauce
1 Tbsp. cornstarch
1 med. pineapple
¼ c. light rum
¼ c. maraschino cherries
   (optional)
¼ c. green grapes (optional)

Cut pineapple in half, including leaves and remove pineapple from inside. Remove woody core and cut remaining fruit into uniform chunks. Cook chicken breast (6 minutes per pound) at 100% power, on rack. Baste with teriyaki sauce during standing time. Toss pineapple with nuts, oranges, cherries, grapes, marmalade and remaining teriyaki/cornstarch sauce. Blend in chunked chicken and place in pineapple halves. Place on flat dish or tray, cover with waxed paper and microwave for 6 - 10 minutes at 100% power until pineapple is hot and sauce thickened. Measure rum into glass measure and microwave for 25 seconds at 100% power. Remove 1 metal tablespoonful of rum and pour the rest of rum over pineapple. Ignite rum in spoon and pour over pineapple to flame. Serve immediately.

After you see how easy it is to "flame" dishes microwave style you'll want to do it as often as possible for a spectacular treat for your guests and family.

TACO SALAD

1 lb. ground beef
1 med. onion, chopped
1 can (15 oz.) kidney beans,
   drained
½ c. water
1 pkg. (1¼ oz.) taco seasoning
   mix
½ med. head lettuce, torn into
   bite sized pieces

2 med. tomatoes, chunked
½ med. green pepper, chopped
½ c. Cheddar cheese, shredded
½ c. Monterey Jack cheese,
   shredded
1 c. broken corn chips

In cook/drain container crumble beef and onion. Microwave for 4½ - 6 minutes at 100% power, stirring once. Into meat stir beans, water and seasoning. Microwave uncovered at 50% power for 10 - 13 minutes until thick and bubbly. While meat mixture is cooking, combine lettuce, tomatoes, green pepper in salad bowl. Spoon hot mixture over lettuce and top with cheese and corn chips. Serve immediately. Pass taco sauce if desired.

CHICKEN CHEDDAR SANDWICH

2 c. chopped cooked chicken
½ c. salad dressing
½ c. pitted ripe olives, chopped
½ c. (2 oz.) sharp Cheddar
    cheese, shredded

¼ c. chopped green pepper
¼ c. chopped onion
6 croissants, split
Lettuce, optional

Cook chicken on rack, covered with paper towel for 6 minutes per pound. Allow chicken to stand and cool and then chop. Combine chicken, salad dressing, olives, cheese and vegetables. Mix lightly. Chill. Fill croissants with lettuce and chicken mixture.

SANDWICHES

CHEESE FRANKS

1 pkg. franks (hotdogs)
Cheddar cheese, shredded
8 - 10 slices bacon

Barbecue sauce
Pickle relish, optional*

     Split franks lengthwise almost in half and to within one inch of the ends. Stuff with cheese. Cook bacon strips on rack for a minute or two until partially done. Brush hotdogs with barbecue sauce and wrap each one in slice of bacon. Secure with toothpick. Cook at 100% power for 1 - 3 minutes per hotdog until cheese is melted and bacon to desired crispness.* Pickle relish may be mixed with cheese if desired before stuffing. Remove toothpicks and place on bun to serve.

MUNCH POCKET SANDWICHES

Pocket bread
Dijon mustard
Tofu, drained

Alfalfa sprouts
Tomato slices
Cheddar cheese, grated

     Cut bread in half and open each half to form a pocket. Spread one side with mustard and take 2 Tbsp. of tofu and spread on each half. Add ⅓ c. of sprouts and 2 slices of tomato to each half. Sprinkle with grated cheese. Microwave at 100% power uncovered, for about 15 seconds per pocket or until warm.

SLOPPY JOES

1 lb. ground beef
½ c. chopped onion
⅓ c. catsup
1 Tbsp. brown sugar
2 tsp. vinegar

1 tsp. prepared mustard
½ tsp. Worcestershire sauce
½ tsp. salt
4 hamburger buns

     Combine onion and beef in cook and drain container. Cook at 100% power for 3 - 5 minutes, stirring once or twice to crumble the beef. Place onion and drained hamburger in 2 quart container and add the remaining ingredients except for the buns. Blend well and heat at 100% power for about 3 more minutes until heated through. Spoon meat mixture into buns and serve.

notes:

Fruits and Vegetables

BUY GOOD FOOD . . .
WHAT YOU SHOULD KNOW!

Fruits and Vegetables

1. Choose beautiful vegetables and fruits. Bright in color, firm texture.
2. Bruises, spots, cuts cause rapid decay so avoid damaged vegetables and fruits. A trace of sweet scent is a sure sign of good quality in fruit.
3. Many vegetables toughen as they mature so choose smaller vegetables to get the youngest, most tender textured.
4. Enzymes alter vegetable flavors as well as texture. Vegetables have less sugar and more starch, therefore less intense flavor and become blander during storage.

Storing Fruits and Vegetables

Most vegetables such as asparagus, celery, peas, spinach do well when put fresh, *unwashed* vegetable in plastic bag or container. This creates small damp environment, humidified by the vegetables own moisture. A vegetable that is actually wet is receptive to bacterial growth and spoilage.

A number of vegetables like potatoes and onions don't like refrigeration. They thrive on higher temperature and lower humidity. Potatoes and onions should not be stored next to one another as each exudes a different gas that shortens the storage life of the other. For longer life, potatoes can be stored in refrigerator which converts starch to sugar, changing the flavor. If you remember to leave at room temperature for a day or two so sugar will reconvert to starch.

Most fruits can be washed and dried before they are put away. However, wash berries and cherries right before serving as too much moisture will hasten decay.

Ripen fruits quickly by placing the unripe fruit in a brown bag with end closed loosely or poked full of small holes. Set on cool shelf and check fruit every day.

FRUITS AND VEGETABLES

FRUITS

BAKED APPLE OR PEAR

2 apples or pears
2 Tbsp. brown sugar
1 Tbsp. butter

½ tsp. cinnamon
Cranberries, optional

Core or half fruit. Place sugar, butter, spices and cranberries in cavities. Place in cups or dish in circle fashion. Cover tightly and cook as follows: 2 apples = 2½ - 4½ min. at 100% power; 4 apples 4 - 6½ min. at 100% power. Rotate after 2 minutes.

BING CHERRY COMPOTE

1 lb. fresh Bing cherries
½ c. red or black currant jelly

¼ c. orange or favorite kind of liqueur

Pit cherries and place in serving dish. Place jelly and liqueur in measuring cup and cook 1 - 1½ minutes covered at 100% power. Let stand a couple of minutes, stir and pour over cherries, mixing gently. Refrigerate at least 4 - 6 hours before serving. This can be used as a dessert too.

CRANBERRY SAUCE

1 lb. fresh cranberries
1 c. sugar
½ tsp. cinnamon, optional

1 (6 oz.) can frozen orange juice concentrate

Place cranberries in ring mold. In a measuring cup defrost juice, add sugar and microwave for 2 minutes at 100% power. Pour over berries, cover with plastic wrap and microwave for 5 minutes at 100% power. I precook the sauce before adding it to the cranberries. By doing this, the berries won't overcook and become mushy while the sauce is heating up. Also, this shortens the cooking time.

FRUIT COMPOTE

1 c. sliced pears*
1 c. sliced peaches*
1 c. canned pitted cherries, drained
1 c. canned pineapple chunks, drained

1 banana, optional*
¼ c. orange juice concentrate
¾ c. brown sugar
¾ tsp. curry, optional
Lemon juice

Combine orange concentrate, brown sugar and curry in 2 cup measure and microwave at 100% power for 2 minutes or until hot. Drain the canned fruit and cut fresh fruit into uniform pieces. (If other fruit used, size of pieces determined by denseness. Dense = small pieces; porous = large pieces.) Combine fruit in 1½ quart bowl with liquid. Cover with plastic wrap and cook at 100% power for 3 - 6 minutes, stirring once. Remove and let stand for 2 minutes before serving. Serve warm or cold.

*Fresh fruit may be brushed with lemon juice to prevent discoloring.

This recipe shows the successful use of the microwave in combining fresh and canned fruits. Just remember the more dense the fresh fruit, the smaller the piece must be. The more porous the fruit, the larger the piece. By using this method neither fresh nor canned will overcook, even though cooked together.

CURRIED FRUIT

2 c. (16 oz.) fruit for salads,
    drained
1 c. dark cherries
1 c. pineapple chunks
1 large banana, chunked

⅓ c. brown sugar
¼ c. flour
1 - 2 tsp. curry powder
¼ c. butter, melted
¼ c. coconut, optional

Drain fruit and mix together with chunked banana. Mix brown sugar, flour and curry and sprinkle over top. Melt butter and drizzle over fruit. Cook 10 minutes at 100% power, uncovered. Coconut may be added last 5 minutes if desired.

HOT MUSTARD PEACHES

1 (29 oz.) can cling peach halves
1 Tbsp. paprika
¾ tsp. salt
1 tsp. finely chopped garlic

½ tsp. cayenne pepper
2 Tbsp. spicy brown mustard
1 tsp. tarragon vinegar
½ c. olive oil

Drain peaches; reserve liquid. In blender container place spices and vinegar; blend until smooth adding about ¼ cup of oil, if needed. With blender running slowly add remaining oil. Pour over peaches. Cover and refrigerate for at least 3 hours. Serve peaches cold or warm gently in microwave (50%) and serve with ham, beef or poultry. Serve extra sauce over meat. 6 - 8 servings. As in this recipe, your condiment section of your grocery store will produce many exciting flavors for basting and adding to recipes if you will let your imagination go. Try a new ingredient every month ... it makes cooking so much more fun!

VEGETABLES

ARTICHOKES WITH SOUR CREAM AND HORSERADISH SAUCE

1 or 2 artichokes
Basil
¼ c. sour cream with chives
1 tsp. lemon juice

Thyme
Garlic powder
½ - ¾ tsp. ground horseradish

Wash artichokes and cut bottom off each one. With scissors trim the tips off of each leaf, about ¾ way up. With a sharp knife trim tip off each artichoke. Place artichokes on rack, sprinkle with herbs and cover tightly with plastic wrap. Cook for 6 - 6½ minutes per pound at 100% power. Allow artichokes to stand while you combine the sour cream, lemon juice and horseradish. Serve artichokes with sauce.

ASPARAGUS SPEARS WITH WINE BUTTER

Fresh asparagus
2 Tbsp. butter
1 Tbsp. white wine

Spices (your favorite)
Salt, if desired*
Nuts, optional

Place asparagus on baking dish (round or oval best) stems to outside. Sprinkle with favorite spices (not salt) and cover tightly with plastic wrap. Cook for 6 - 6½ minutes per pound at 100% power. In 1 cup measure place butter and microwave for 30 - 45 seconds at 100% power until melted. Stir in wine. Pour sauce over asparagus and top with nuts, sunflower nuts, etc. *Add salt to asparagus during standing time if needed. Remember when vegetables are cooked in microwave, relate methods to conventional methods. Steaming in conventional cooking is best (covered tightly, hot heat). Therefore, covered with plastic (our "covered tightly" lid) at 100% power is best in the microwave. Just always ask yourself ... "How do I cook that in conventional cooking" and do it the same way. This goes for all microwave cooking.

BROCCOLI ALMONDINE WITH HOT POPPY SEED SAUCE

1 stalk fresh broccoli
¼ c. almonds

½ tsp. savory
½ tsp. basil

Sauce:

3 Tbsp. butter
2 Tbsp. lemon juice
1 tsp. sugar

Dash salt
Dash hot pepper sauce
½ tsp. poppy seed

Break or cut broccoli into uniform pieces leaving the flowerets in larger pieces than the stalk. Place stalk pieces around the outside edge of round serving bowl or platter. Place flowerets in the middle, stalks pointing outward. Top with savory and basil. Sprinkle with almonds. Cover with plastic wrap and cook for 6 minutes per pound. While vegetable is standing melt butter in 1 cup measure for 45 seconds at 100% power. Blend in remaining ingredients and cook an additional 30 - 60 seconds before pouring over vegetables.

By arranging the dense pieces to the outside of pan where three way cooking (up/down/inward) takes place and more porous in the center where only two way cooking (up/down) takes place ... all vegetables parts will come out evenly cooked ... not overdone ... and all at the same time. This method of proper arrangement with all vegetables is very successful for even cooking.

BROCCOLI CASSEROLE

3 Tbsp. oil, optional
½ c. chopped onion
2 (10 oz.) pkg. frozen chopped
    broccoli, defrosted and
    drained
6 slices American cheese

1 (10¾ oz.) can cream of
    mushroom soup, undiluted
1½ c. bread crumbs
½ c. butter or margarine
Dash salt and pepper, optional
Paprika

Saute onion in 1½ qt. dish for 2 - 3 minutes at 100% power. Add broccoli, cover with waxed paper and cook for 6 - 7 minutes at 100% power. Stir once or twice to break up. Spoon half of broccoli mixture into a 2 qt. casserole. Layer with ½ the cheese and ½ the soup. Combine bread crumbs with melted butter and layer ½ the crumbs over the soup. Repeat layers, topping with bread crumbs. Sprinkle with paprika, cover with waxed paper and cook for 8 minutes at 100% power. Turn only if uneven cooking.

BROCCOLI STUFFED TOMATOES

1 pkg. (10 oz.) frozen chopped
    broccoli
2 Tbsp. chopped onion
¼ c. salad dressing
¼ tsp. tarragon

⅛ tsp. salt
4 oz. Monterey Jack cheese, cut
    into 6 slices
4 med. sized ripe tomatoes

Thaw and drain broccoli. Cook for 2 - 3 minutes at 100% power and set aside. Microwave onion, covered at 100% power for about 1 minute. Mix with broccoli, salad dressing and seasonings. Core tomatoes and slice each in half horizontally. Arrange cut side up on glass serving plate* and spoon broccoli mixture onto each. Microwave uncovered for 4½ - 5 minutes at 100% power, until heated through. Top with cheese slices and microwave uncovered at 50 - 70% power for 1 - 3 minutes until cheese is melted. Serve hot.

*Use cup cake cooker if available.

BRUSSELS SPROUTS CASSEROLE

2 lbs. fresh Brussels sprouts*
1 med. onion, sliced in rings
1/2 - 3/4 c. each Romano, Swiss
    and Cheddar cheese

Cayenne pepper
1/2 tsp. salt
1/2 c. white wine
1/4 c. dry crumbs

Cook Brussels sprouts and onion in ring mold, covered, at 100% power for 6 - 8 minutes. Drain and set aside. In 1 1/2 quart shallow baking dish layer 1/2 sprouts and 1/2 onion. Sprinkle with half of cheese. Sprinkle with cayenne and salt. Repeat and pour wine over this. Sprinkle with crumbs. Bake uncovered at 70% power for 10 - 15 minutes. *May use frozen sprouts which have been defrosted and cooked for 4 - 6 minutes at 100% power.

Overripe bananas may be frozen for 3 - 4 months to be used later. One teaspoon of lemon juice per cup of banana helps minimize color change.

CARROTS AU GRATIN

1 lb. carrots, sliced
1/2 c. minced onion
1 c. milk
2 Tbsp. flour
1/2 tsp. dry mustard
1/2 tsp. celery salt

1/2 tsp. parsley
1/4 tsp. salt
Dash white pepper
3 oz. cheese slices
1/2 c. bread crumbs
Paprika

Spread carrots evenly in ring mold. Cover and cook at 100% power for 5 - 6 minutes. Set aside. In 4 cup measure saute or cook onion, covered, for 1 1/2 minutes at 100% power. Stir in flour and spices except for salt. Slowly add milk. Cook for 4 - 6 minutes at 70% power until thick, stirring once or twice. Add salt. Place half of carrots on bottom of round 1 to 1 1/2 quart dish. Cover with cheese slices. Add remaining carrots and top with white sauce and crumbs. Sprinkle with paprika and cook uncovered for 3 minutes at 100% power. This casserole can be cooked on high power since the cheese is "buried" and there is no prolonged cooking time. If there were, you would have to lower temperature as you would conventionally, to prevent cheese from becoming stringy.

FROSTED CAULIFLOWER

1 med. head cauliflower	1 tsp. dry mustard (optional)
½ c. mayonnaise	¾ c. grated sharp Cheddar
¼ tsp. salt	cheese
1 - 2 tsp. prepared mustard	Paprika

Remove woody base of cauliflower, but leave whole. Aerate base with knife to make more porous.* Place in 1½ qt. glass dish and cook covered for 6 minutes per pound. Rest covered 5 minutes. Season cauliflower, if desired. In 2 cup container mix mayonnaise, salt and mustard. Heat 45 seconds to 1 minute, uncovered, at 70% power. Spread over cauliflower and sprinkle with grated cheese. Heat 1 minute or until cheese melts at about 70% power. Sprinkle with paprika. *By perforating the base or core of any dense vegetable, you can get a "porous" effect to speed the cooking.

SCALLOPED EGGPLANT

1 large (1½ lb.) eggplant, peeled and diced into ½" cubes	⅓ c. milk
	1 egg
⅓ c. chopped onion	1 tsp. salt
⅓ c. butter or margarine	¼ tsp. white pepper
1¼ c. seasoned herbed dressing, divided	¼ tsp. Greek seasoning, optional
1 (10¾ oz.) can cream of mushroom soup	½ c. grated Cheddar cheese

Place eggplant and onion in a 2 quart container, covered, and cook on 100% power for about 8 minutes.* Place dressing in 2 cup measure, top with butter and cook at 100% power for 1 minute. Stir well and reserve ¼ cup of topping. Mix stuffing, soup, milk, egg which has been slightly beaten and seasonings to the eggplant/onion mixture. Mix well and sprinkle with remaining dressing and cheese. Microwave for about 7 - 8 minutes at 70% power or until very hot and cheese melted. Leave this uncovered as you want as crusty a top like you would in conventional cooking for a casserole of this type. Therefore, you use similar techniques, no cover and medium high heat. *It is not necessary to add butter when you saute vegetables in the microwave except as flavoring which is added at the end of cooking, if desired ... and a little bit goes a long ways.

LIMA BEANS AND BROCCOLI CASSEROLE

1 pkg. (10 oz.) frozen lima beans	¼ - ½ tsp. salt
1 pkg. (10 oz.) frozen broccoli	¼ tsp. pepper
1 can condensed mushroom soup	Dash Worcestershire sauce
½ c. buttered bread crumbs	½ c. shredded Cheddar cheese

Defrost vegetables for 5 - 6 minutes at 50% power, drain well. Place lima beans in 1 qt. casserole, cook covered for 1 - 2 minutes at 50% power. Add broccoli, combine with soup and spices. Top with bread crumbs. Cook at 50% power, uncovered, for 10 minutes. Sprinkle with cheese, cook an additional 2 - 5 minutes at 50% power. Lima beans are cooked at a lower temperature for a short time. The bean family, other than green beans, need slow, long cooking times so they won't be hard like "little bullets". Here again we are using similar "thinking" (conventional vs. microwave) and using similar methods for cooking. Remember ... food is food and we must treat it with similar techniques, no matter what cooking method we use.

BAKED POTATO

Use one or more baking potatoes. Place on rack* in circle fashion and cook at 100% power for 6 - 6½ minutes per pound. Wrap in foil and let stand 10 minutes or longer to finish cooking. This is very important. If cooking many potatoes, rearrange half way through cooking time. Potatoes will stay hot for 45 minutes. To rewarm potato or twice baked potato, cook at 100% power for 1 ½ - 2 minutes. *Use cup cake cooker with potatoes in upright position if available. This method is excellent for potatoes and other vegetables. Standing upright is like a TV antenna and attracts the microwaves. This helps vegetables to cook more evenly, not letting the microwaves get trapped on the bottom of the oven under the vegetables like they can if they are lying flat on bottom.

MISSION POTATOES

6 med. potatoes (about 2 lbs.) peeled, sliced ¼" thick	8 oz. Cheddar cheese, shredded
1 med. onion, sliced	1 can (4 oz.) green chilies, seeded and cut into strips
1 clove garlic, chopped	½ c. sour cream at room temp.
1 tsp. salt	1 egg, lightly beaten
1 tsp. instant beef flavored bouillon	Paprika
	Crumbs

Bring ¼ - ½ c. water to boil in 2 qt. casserole. Add potatoes, onion, garlic, salt and bouillon. Cover and cook at 100% power for 10 - 12 minutes until potatoes are almost tender. Pour ½ of potatoes and their liquid into shallow 2 qt. casserole. Cover with half of the cheese and half the chilies. Top with remaining potato mixture and all but 2 Tbsp. of cheese. Cook for 5 minutes covered at 50% power. Remove and spread mixture of sour cream and egg on top. Arrange chilies and cheese on top and sprinkle with crumbs and paprika. Cook an additional 3 minutes at 50% power. Let stand 10 minutes before serving. Think the same way when cooking microwave as conventionally. This recipe is a good example. Cook potatoes covered, on high ... then lower temperature after assembling and adding cheese (just like you would for conventional methods) and leave uncovered so a dryer, more crusty top will occur. Just always remember ... Think conventionally and use the same techniques when microwaving!

FABULOUS STUFFED POTATOES

4 med. baking potatoes
1 c. (8 oz.) sour cream & chives
½ tsp. salt
⅛ tsp. pepper
½ tsp. Beau Monde seasoning
⅛ tsp. Greek seasoning
1 (8 oz.) can sliced mushrooms, drained

¼ c. chopped green onion
¼ c. butter
¼ c. shredded Cheddar cheese, optional
¼ c. buttered bread crumbs
¼ c. milk

Bake potatoes according to directions for Baked Potatoes. Cut hot potatoes in half lengthwise and carefully scoop out pulp. Beat with electric mixer until smooth. Add cream, salt, pepper and spices. Beat until fluffy. Heat milk for 1 minute at 100% power or until hot. Gradually add to potatoes. Saute mushrooms and onion in butter for 3 minutes at 100% power and fold into potato mixture. Fill potato shells and sprinkle with bread crumbs. Place on glass serving platter and microwave at 100% power for 2 - 3 minutes until heated through. If potatoes are not hot but room temperature, cook for 1 - 1½ minutes per potato serving.* These may be made ahead and frozen. *Sprinkle cheese on after cooking if not mixed in and cook an additional 1 minute at 50% power if needed for cheese to melt. Remember when cooking cheese, lower temperatures are needed to keep cheese from stringing.

OVEN BROWNED POTATOES

2 Tbsp. fat or roast drippings
½ tsp. browning sauce
¼ tsp. paprika

¼ tsp. herb of your choice (thyme, basil, etc.)
4 - 6 med. sized potatoes, peeled

In 1½ quart container, place butter, drippings or other fat along with browning sauce, paprika and herbs. Cook for 1 minute at 100% power. Stir well. Roll potatoes in mixture until coated well. Cook covered for 4 minutes. Stir potatoes again and cook uncovered for another 4 - 5 minutes or until potatoes are tender. These may be fixed ahead and left at room temperature. When ready to serve heat for 1 minute, uncovered; stir and heat additional 30 - 45 seconds until hot.

SCALLOPED "RED" POTATOES

½ c. chopped onion
¼ c. chopped green pepper,
   optional
2 Tbsp. butter
2 Tbsp. flour
½ tsp. salt
⅓ tsp. pepper
Dash of garlic powder

2 tsp. instant chicken bouillon
¼ - ½ c. water
1 (8 oz.) can stewed tomatoes
5 c. potatoes, peeled, thinly
   sliced
Parmesan cheese, grated
Paprika

Cook or saute vegetables in butter* for 1½ minutes at 100% power. Blend in flour, seasonings, water, tomatoes and bouillon. Cook for 2 - 4 minutes at 100% power until thickened. Stir once, if necessary. Add potatoes and stir lightly to coat. Cook covered for 10 - 15 minutes at 100% power until potatoes are tender. Stir once, or cook in ring mold. Sprinkle with cheese and paprika. Allow to stand a few minutes, uncovered, before serving.

*If you wish to "saute" without the added calories of the butter, you can. Just add ¼ - ½ tsp. of butter during standing time (or none if you prefer). You'll get the butter flavor from that small amount without the added calories.

HAWAIIAN SWEET POTATOES

1 can (16 oz.) yams or sweet
   potatoes, drained
1 small banana, sliced
1 tsp. lemon juice
⅓ c. orange juice

½ tsp. salt
Dash pepper
¼ c. whole pecans
2 Tbsp. flaked coconut, toasted
Dash cinnamon, optional

Place sweet potatoes and bananas in 1 qt. casserole. Baste generously with combination of orange juice, lemon juice and spices. Top with pecans and coconut. Cover tightly and microwave for 5 - 6 minutes at 100% power. If you use fresh sweet potatoes instead of canned, cook them according to the directions for baked potatoes in this book. Sweet potatoes have a bit more sugar than white, therefore they will cook a bit faster than white potatoes. Otherwise, the technique is the same. Let cool, then use as you would canned.

SPINACH AND ARTICHOKE HEARTS

2 tsp. instant beef bouillon
3 (10 oz.) pkgs. frozen chopped
   spinach
½ tsp. salt
¼ tsp. black pepper
¼ tsp. Tabasco

⅛ tsp. nutmeg
½ pint sour cream
1 (8 oz.) can artichoke hearts,
   drained and quartered
2 Tbsp. margarine

Defrost spinach and drain. Place in 3 quart casserole, sprinkle with bouillon. Cover and cook for 7 - 10 minutes until tender. Add spices and Tabasco. Fold in sour cream and artichokes. Dot with margarine and cook, covered for additional 6 - 8 minutes at 70 - 80% power.

SPINACH WITH GARLIC

2 lbs. fresh spinach	½ tsp. pepper
6 cloves garlic, minced	¼ tsp. nutmeg, optional
¼ tsp. salt	¼ c. olive oil

Clean spinach well. Discard large stems and place spinach dripping wet into a 3 quart container. (Since there is so much water in vegetables, naturally, you won't need to add more water to cook properly.) Cover tightly and cook at 100% power for 10 minutes, stirring half way through. While the spinach is cooking mince the garlic and put in with spinach when you stir, half way through cooking. Next, add the spices and toss with olive oil. Cover and cook another 1 - 2 minutes at 100% power until flavors mingle. You will notice that the total cooking time of 12 minutes equals the 6 minutes per lb. that I refer to so often when estimating cooking times for vegetables, meats, etc. This lets you use the vegetable of your choice and still know how long to cook it without following a recipe, using the 6 minutes per lb. base.

ACORN SQUASH WITH APPLE AND RAISIN GLAZE

2 med. acorn squash	2 Tbsp. brown sugar
1 med. apple, sliced	¼ tsp. nutmeg
2 Tbsp. raisins	2 Tbsp. butter
¼ c. orange juice	

Microwave squash for 5 - 6 minutes per pound at 100% power. Half way through cooking time cut squash open and remove seeds. Cover squash or put back together with rubber bands and continue cooking the remainder of the time. Arrange apple slices in petal design on top of squash with raisins in middle and baste thoroughly with sauce made from orange juice, brown sugar, spices and butter. Microwave uncovered for 4 - 5 minutes at 100% power until sauce is bubbly.

"MORELLE" SQUASH

2 lbs. yellow squash, sliced	2 Tbsp. butter
1 c. chopped onion	1 Tbsp. sugar
1 tsp. butter	1½ tsp. salt
2 eggs, beaten	½ c. Mozzarella cheese
½ c. sour cream	½ c. ground almonds, optional*

Place squash and onions in ring mold or 2 quart container. Cover and cook 6 minutes per pound at 100%. Drain vegetables and dot 1 tsp. butter. Mash. Mix together eggs, cream, rest of butter, sugar, spices and cheese. Stir into the squash and microwave for 6 - 8 minutes at 70% power. Sprinkle with almonds *or use crumbs if desired. Cook 1 minute more. I've lowered the heat for the final cooking because of the dairy products in the recipe.

SPAGHETTI SQUASH WITH TOMATO SAUCE

1 spaghetti squash
1 (10 oz.) jar tomato or spaghetti
   sauce (homemade may be
   substituted)

Parsley
Parmesan cheese

Weigh squash. Set upright in small bowl so squash may stand during cooking. Cook 6 minutes per pound at 100% power*. Allow to stand for a while to finish cooking. Heat sauce during standing time. With fork, pull out squash, spaghetti style and top with tomato sauce, Parmesan and parsley. *Cook squash one-half of cooking time, then cut in half and scoop out seeds. Place together again with rubber bands and finish cooking. The upright position attracts microwaves as an antenna and allows them to enter foods evenly in all directions instead of letting them "trap" on the bottom of the microwave as they do under a large piece lying on the bottom of the oven.

OLD ITALY TOMATOES

¾ c. (3 oz.) shredded Mozzarella
   cheese
2 Tbsp. finely chopped
   pepperoni
1 green onion, chopped

2 Tbsp. mayonnaise
¼ tsp. basil leaves
¼ tsp. oregano
2 med. tomatoes

Combine cheese, pepperoni, onion, mayonnaise and seasonings in bowl and mix well. Slice each tomato into four slices and place in circle on glass serving plate.* Spoon cheese mixture onto each and spread to cover completely. Microwave uncovered at 70% power for 3 - 5 minutes until cheese is melted. *Use cupcake cooker if available. This keeps tomatoes from tipping over and also keeps them well separated and in circle position for more even cooking.

SPICY CREAMED TURNIPS

2 lbs. turnips, peeled, cut into
    cubes
½ onion, cubed
¼ c. butter
⅓ c. flour
1½ c. milk
1 - 2 Tbsp. white wine

2 - 3 tsp. Dijon mustard
Dash Worcestershire sauce
¼ tsp. salt
⅛ tsp. hot pepper sauce
½ - ¾ c. shredded sharp
    Cheddar cheese (optional)
Crumbs

    Place turnips and onion in large circle baker. Cover and cook 5 - 6 minutes per pound at 100% power. Drain well. In the meantime melt butter in 4 cup measure, add flour and cook for about 1 minute to reduce flour taste. Add reserved liquid and cook from 70 - 100% power about 2 - 3 minutes until mixture boils. Reduce power and simmer about 1 minute. Stir in mustard, Worcestershire sauce and spices. Stir sauce into vegetables. Cover and refrigerate for 1 - 2 days, if possible before serving. When ready to serve, cook at 50% power for about 15 minutes until very hot. Sprinkle with cheese and crumbs and cook, uncovered, for an additional 2 - 4 minutes. This is rich, good and very different. The key, however, is letting it stand a day or two so flavors will blend.

VEGETABLES EXTRAVAGANZA

1 head cauliflower
4 - 6 whole med. sized onions
¼ - ½ lb. spinach

2 - 3 beets, shredded
Spices

    Aerate cauliflower base with knife, season with favorite spices. Place cauliflower in center of large round platter, make a circle of onions around it leaving space in between each onion. Cook at 100% power, covered with plastic wrap for 5 - 5½ min. per lb. Uncover and place nests of spinach topped with shredded beet between each onion, sprinkle with spices, cover, cook additional 2 - 5 minutes to cook added vegetables. This is a simple but spectacular dish. Just remember your 6 min. per lb. total weight cooking time. Use part of this time to precook the more dense foods before adding the porous, more easily cooked items for the remaining time. If the porous vegetables were in the center of the plate, pre-cooking would not be necessary. In this case they are not, so we precook so they will not become overcooked while the dense vegetables cook.

VEGETABLE MEDLEY

Assorted vegetables
   (cauliflower, broccoli,
   zucchini, squash,
   mushrooms, onion, green
   or red pepper, etc.,
   whatever in season)

¼ c. butter
Lemon pepper
Thyme
Paprika
Basil

Arrange cleaned vegetables on a 12 - 14" glass plate in attractive color-ful arrangement according to denseness of vegetables (hardest or most dense to outside of plate to softest or most porous in center). Sprinkle lightly with herbs and cover tightly with plastic wrap. Microwave for 6 minutes per pound at 100% power. Drain liquid from plate after standing time, if necessary. Melt but-ter and mix with lemon pepper. Pour over vegetables and serve. When cooking vegetables always ask yourself ... "Is vegetable dense or porous?" Dense takes a full 6 minutes per pound to cook ... porous may take less. Also large pieces will take longer than smaller pieces to cook. Consider these things when cooking all types of vegetables, but always use a 6 minutes per pound as a starting basis.

ZUCCHINI SOUFFLE

2 lbs. sliced zucchini
1 Tbsp. butter, optional
⅔ c. sour cream
⅓ c. grated Cheddar cheese
½ tsp. salt
¼ tsp. seasoning salt or garlic
   salt

⅛ tsp. paprika
½ tsp. basil
1 egg yolk, beaten
1 Tbsp. chopped chives
1 egg white
½ c. cracker crumbs
2 Tbsp. butter

Cook zucchini for 6 minutes per pound, covered. (A ring mold will make it so you won't have to stir.) Drain. Melt 1 Tbsp. butter in 2 cup measure. Stir in sour cream, cheese and spices. Microwave at 50% power for 2 - 3 minutes until warm and cheese is melted. Remove from heat and stir in egg yolk and chives. Stir into zucchini and fold in egg white. Place in souffle dish. Toss crumbs with melted butter. Sprinkle on top of casserole. Microwave uncovered for 3 - 5 min-utes at 70% power.

ZUCCHINI AND TOMATOES

2 c. thinly sliced zucchini
½ tsp. basil
½ tsp. Greek seasoning

1½ c. coarsely chopped
   tomatoes
Parmesan cheese

Weigh vegetables. Combine vegetables and seasonings and place in ring mold. Cover tightly with plastic wrap and cook for 6 - 6½ min. per pound. Sprinkle generously with Parmesan cheese during standing time and allow

53

vegetables to stand until cheese melts. Vegetables may also be arranged on round tray, zucchini to outside and tomatoes inside, stirring together during standing time. If a ring mold is not used, the zucchini to the outside and tomatoes to the inside is used because the zucchini takes longer (more dense) than the tomatoes and by arranging in this manner, will get heavier microwave concentration (3 way) while the tomatoes get less (2 way), therefore arriving at doneness at the same time.

notes:

_____
_____
_____
_____
_____
_____
_____
_____
_____
_____
_____
_____
_____
_____
_____
_____
_____
_____
_____
_____
_____
_____
_____
_____
_____
_____

Entrées

DEALING IN MULTIPLES WHEN COOKING IN THE MICROWAVE

When the Six Minute per Pound Rule which is discussed in Basic Precepts of Meats on page 55 is not used, the following rules should apply when cooking multiples.

Individual Food Items

1. Determine the time for cooking *one* food item such as a piece of chicken, potato or corn-on-the-cob, etc.

2. Double the time to cook two pieces of the chosen food.

3. To increase the items by more than two, *double* second item and for each additional piece of food added use only *one-half* of the cooking time of the first item.

   Example: One corn-on-the cob = 3 minutes
   Two corn-on-the cob = 6 minutes (time doubled)
   Three corn-on-the cob = 7½ minutes or First Item + Time Doubled for Second Item + ½ First item for Third item ...
   (This can be carried on for more items also.)

Foods Made By Recipe

1. Cook recipe by time given in cookbook.

2. When doubling a recipe for a casserole, soup, etc., add *one-half* of the cooking time for the original amount.

   Example: Time First Recipe + ½ Time First Recipe = 1½ Time First Recipe

ENTREES

BASIC PRECEPTS OF MEAT COOKERY

When cooking meat, similar methods used in conventional cooking should be applied to microwave cooking. Food is food and we must treat it the same no matter what cooking vehicle we use.

TENDER CUTS

Hotter temperatures (70% ... large pieces; 100% ... small pieces). Cook on rack. No cover required (wax paper or paper towel may be used to help retain some moisture and heat on larger cuts). Uniform size (try to stay away from irregular shapes and thicknesses). Similar cooking methods as conventional. (For example: In conventional cooking, a standing rib roast is cooked on a rack, uncovered in a hot oven.)

LESS TENDER CUTS

Lower temperatures (30% preferred). Moisture added. Roasts depend on slow cooking process and the liquid to soften and tenderize connective tissue. Covered or cooking bag. Uniform size (again, try to stay away from irregular shapes and thicknesses). Turn several times during cooking. Similar cooking methods as conventional (ask yourself: When cooking conventionally do I cover? Add liquid? Use high heat? Use low heat? You will do it just the same in the microwave).

RELATING MICROWAVE COOKING TEMPERATURES TO CONVENTIONAL COOKING TEMPERATURES

When trying to compare your microwave and your conventional temperatures, think of your oven dial which goes from 500 to 150 degrees and your microwave. Correlate them as follows:

100% power = 475 - 500 degrees; deep fat fry or broil.
70% power = 350 - 375 degrees
50% power = 300 - 350 degrees
30% power = 250 - 300 degrees
10% power = 150 degrees or as low as you can turn the burner on top of your stove without it going off.

Choose the same temperature to cook your food in the microwave as the recipe suggests you would when cooking conventionally. The above chart will help you relate the two methods so you may choose the right temperature or power level. Simply follow your conventional recipes and convert temperatures to microwave power levels ... Think conventionally ... cook at the same temperatures.

LOWERING COOKING TEMPERATURES

Six minutes a pound will cook most all foods (meat or vegetables) that are in a solid piece to well done. Of course smaller, more porous pieces of food will take less time than the solid, dense pieces, but the 6 minutes per pound is your base starting point. As in conventional cooking, different foods take different temperatures. Below is the technique for lowering your temperature in the microwave to cook to well done.

100% power = 6 min. per lb.
90% power = 7 min. per lb.
80% power = 8 min. per lb.
70% power = 9 min. per lb.
60% power = 10 min. per lb.
50% power = 11 min. per lb.
40% power = 12 min. per lb.
30% power = 13 min. per lb.
20% power = 14 min. per lb.
10% power = 15 min. per lb.

VARIOUS DEGREES OF DONENESS

For meats that you wish done to various stages (rare to well done) such as tender and semi-tender roasts, steaks and chops the time is as follows: 100% = 6 min. for well done; 5 min. for medium; 4 min. for rare.

You may also want to lower the temperatures and still achieve different degrees of doneness. The method is as follows: Degree of doneness desired = medium (5 min. a pound at 100%). Therefore, you use the same table as above for lowering temperatures, but substituting your degree of doneness at the top of the scale opposite 100% power and continuing to lower the temperatures as above. For example:

100% power = 5 min. per lb. (medium)
90% power = 6 min. per lb.
80% power = 7 min. per lb.

and so forth down the scale.

For less tender cuts (roasts and larger cuts) you will find that you need to cook by the slow simmer method. It takes liquid to break down the connective tissue in less tender meats. Therefore, it is important to cook a long time at a low temperature, 22 - 45 minutes per lb. at 25 - 30% power, turning every 30 - 45 minutes, in a cooking bag with liquids added. This is the best way for cooking pork roasts to insure complete cooking safety as you will get even heat doing it this way.

STANDING TIME

On all microwave cooking of meat and poultry, 20 - 25% of total cooking takes place after the oven shuts off. This is a process that takes place whether you want or not. Therefore, you must learn to allow for this time or STANDING TIME. Check large pieces of meat, or poultry in several spots with your thermometer to assure that proper temperatures are reached. Temperatures will rise 10 - 15 degrees during standing time so you must undercook by that amount to achieve the final temperature. For example:

Rare = 130 degrees before standing, 140 degrees after standing
Medium = 150 degrees before standing, 160 degrees after standing
Well = 160 degrees before standing, 170 degrees after standing

As you can see we must undercook by 20% to allow for this. Therefore our food is 80% done when our microwave turns off. I have allowed for this in 6 minutes per lb. rule. We then "tent" or cover the meat with aluminum foil to help cooking procedure to continue and heat to distribute evenly.

Also, do remember that meats with natural fats brown if cooked longer than 10 minutes. Fat will rise to surface and caramelize.

BEEF

MEAL IN DISH VARIATION

¼ c. stuffing mix
¼ lb. beef pattie
¼ - ½ c. frozen broccoli,
    defrosted
Horseradish
Soy sauce

2 mushrooms and parsley
Tomato slice
Spices (dill, pepper, paprika,
    basil, parsley, etc.), at least
    two

Place a thin layer of dry stuffing mix in bottom of individual au gratin dish. Top stuffing with a layer of defrosted and drained chopped broccoli. On top of this place the beef pattie and brush with horseradish and soy sauce mixture. Sprinkle with mushrooms and parsley. Top with tomato slice (fruit slice may be substituted). Sprinkle with spices and cover tightly with plastic wrap. Microwave for 3 - 4 minutes at 100% power. If salt is used, salt during standing time. (This recipe is only a guide. You may use any type of meat, vegetables or fruit as well as different sauces.)

MARINATED KABOBS

1½ - 2 lb. beef or lamb, chunked
    into 1 inch cubes
¼ c. cooking oil
1 Tbsp. vinegar
1 tsp. instant onion flakes
1 tsp. garlic powder

3 med. carrots, 1 inch chunks
Pineapple chunks
1 jar whole onions, drained
1 c. fresh mushrooms
Browning powder

Place cubes in plastic bag and marinate in oil, vinegar, onion and garlic for overnight or several days. When ready to fix kabobs, combine carrots in 1 qt. and microwave covered for 5 - 5½ minutes per pound, until nearly done. Let stand. Coat meat cubes with browning powder and thread meat, carrots, pineapple, onions and mushrooms onto 10 inch skewers. Place kabobs on rack or rice rack. Cover with waxed paper and microwave for 8 - 10 minutes at 100% power or to desired doneness, rearranging once for even cooking.

HAMBURGER PATTIES

1 lb. lean ground beef
Browning seasoning mix
    (homemade or commercial)

Shape beef into 4 (4 oz.) patties and flatten to about ½ inch in thickness. They should be about 4½ - 5 inch in diameter. Make a small hole about the size of a nickel in the center of each. This will make the burger get four way cooking since the microwaves can enter from each side (inside/outside and up/down). The edges won't have to be overdone in order to cook the center. Sprinkle with browning after you dampen the meat slightly. Place burgers on rack, in a circle arrangement, and cook covered with waxed paper for 1 min. 15 seconds for one patty, turning after 45 seconds or 4 min. 30 seconds for 4 patties, also turning half way through the time. Let stand after turning back to original side for a minute or two before serving. Hamburger doesn't take the full 6 minutes per pound because it is made up of many little pieces instead of the solid piece that takes the 6 minutes per pound to cook to doneness. The more pieces per pound, the shorter the cooking time.

HAMBURGER TOPPINGS

Hawaiian Topping:

1 (3 oz.) pkg. cream cheese,
    softened
2 Tbsp. pineapple juice

⅛ tsp. powdered sugar
Pineapple slices

Combine cheese, juice and ginger. Beat until fluffy. Cook the pineapple slices on top of hamburger while cooking. Divide topping evenly over finished patties.

Cheese Zip Topping:

1 (3 oz.) pkg. cream cheese,
softened
1 tsp. Worcestershire sauce
1 Tbsp. grated onion

1 Tbsp. finely chopped green
pepper - 1 to 2 Tbsp.
horseradish

Combine horseradish and cheese with Worcestershire sauce and beat until fluffy. Add remaining ingredients and spoon over cooked burgers.

Pizza Topping:

⅓ c. sliced stuffed green olives
⅓ c. sliced pitted ripe olives

½ c. pizza sauce
1 c. shredded Mozzarella cheese

Combine all ingredients and divide over cooked burger.

Swiss Cheese with Bacon:

4 slices bacon
1 c. grated Swiss cheese

½ c. sour cream

Cook bacon according to directions until crisp. Cool and crumble and combine with cheese and cream. Spoon over cooked burger.

Blue Cheese and Sour Cream Topping:

⅓ c. crumbled Blue cheese
⅔ c. sour cream

2 lbs. thinly sliced green onions

Combine all ingredients and divide over cooked burger.

LAYERED MEAT LOAF

2 lbs. ground beef
2 eggs, slightly beaten
1½ c. crushed cracker crumbs
½ c. chopped onion

2 Tbsp. Worcestershire sauce
1½ tsp. salt
½ tsp. pepper
Dash garlic powder

Filling:

8 oz. fresh mushrooms, sliced
1 med. onion, chopped
2 Tbsp. butter, optional
1 tsp. thyme

1 tsp. cumin
1 c. sour cream with chives
1 c. bread crumbs

Mix meatloaf ingredients thoroughly and set aside. Cook mushrooms and onions (in butter if used) for 3 minutes at 100% power, uncovered. Add spices, sour cream and bread crumbs. Spread ⅓ of meat mixture in bottom of bundt pan, top with ½ of filling, ⅓ of meat mixture, rest of filling and then the last ⅓ of meat mixture. Microwave for 5 minutes at 100% power, reduce to

60% power for 10 - 15 minutes or until internal temperature reaches 140%. Rotate while cooking once or twice, if necessary for even cooking. Let stand a few minutes before turning out onto serving dish.

BACON WRAPPED MINI LOAVES

½ c. chopped green pepper
½ c. chopped onion
4 thick slices of bacon
1 lb. lean ground beef
1 slice bread, moistened with 2
    Tbsp. milk and torn into
    pieces
1 egg

2 Tbsp. catsup
½ tsp. salt
⅛ tsp. pepper
1 tsp. horseradish
1 Tbsp. Worcestershire sauce
1½ tsp. curry
¼ tsp. browning sauce or
    powder

Combine vegetables in small cup. Cover and microwave for 1 - 1½ minutes at 100% power. Set aside. Place bacon on double thickness of paper towels. Cover with paper towel and microwave at 100% power for 2 - 3 minutes until slightly underdone. In 4 cup measure combine beef, vegetables and remaining. Blend well. Divide into two equal parts and shape into two 6 x 3 inch loaves and wrap 2 bacon slices around, securing with a toothpick. Place loaves on roasting rack, sprinkle with browning powder, cover with waxed paper and microwave 7 - 11 minutes at 100% power. Rotate once if necessary and allow to stand covered for 3 minutes.

ROLLED MEATLOAF

1½ lbs. ground beef
2 eggs
¼ c. seasoned bread crumbs
1 Tbsp. Worcestershire sauce
1 tsp. horseradish
¾ tsp. salt

½ tsp. Greek seasoning
½ tsp. pepper
½ c. pimento*
½ c. chopped onion*
½ c. chopped green pepper*

Mix ground beef, eggs, crumbs and seasonings. On wax paper form a rectangular base with meat. On meat, sprinkle vegetables which have been cooked at 100% power, covered for 1½ minutes and cooled. Roll meat by lifting waxed paper and rolling meat up, jellyroll fashion. Press end seams together. Place meat, seam side down on roasting rack. Cook 5 minutes at 100% power, uncovered. Reduce power and cook at 50% power for 5 - 12 minutes. Cover to keep warm. Do not overcook as meat will continue to cook during standing time.

*Different stuffing may be used.

BEEF WITH BROCCOLI

1 Tbsp. oil
1 lb. boneless steak, cut into
    thin strips*
1 clove garlic, finely chopped
⅓ tsp. ginger
3 - 4 c. broccoli flowerets
¾ c. sliced fresh mushrooms

½ med. onion, chopped
1 - 2 Tbsp. cornstarch
½ c. beef broth
1 Tbsp. sherry
1 Tbsp. soy sauce
Toasted sesame seeds, optional

Combine garlic, ginger, broth, sherry and soy sauce. Pour over beef and marinate for at least 30 minutes. Drain and reserve marinade to thicken later. In oblong dish heat oil for 2 minutes at 100% power. Stir in beef and heat for 3½ - 4½ min. at 100% power, uncovered, stirring twice. Add broccoli and onions, cover with plastic and heat additional 3 - 4 minutes. Remove cover and add mushrooms. Recover and heat an additional 2 - 3 minutes or until broccoli is crisp tender. Stir in cornstarch blended with liquids. Heat 3 - 4 minutes at 100% power until sauce thickens, stirring once if needed. Top with sesame seeds if desired. (*Sirloin steak is excellent choice of meat.)

BROILED STEAK A LA MICROWAVE
(Rack and browning skillet)

1 (8 oz.) steak*
Thyme
Basil

Pepper
Paprika
Browning spice, if available

Rack: Place steak in dish on meat rack. Season lightly on both sides with seasonings. Cook 6 minutes per pound for well done at 100% power. (Med. approximately 5 min. per pound; rare approximately 4 min. per pound.)

Browning skillet: Place skillet in microwave and heat for 4 - 5 min. at 100% power. While skillet is heating apply spices. Cook in skillet for 1 min. at 100% power. Turn and finish cooking for 1 - 2 min. 100% power until done. Time will be slightly more or less according to desired doneness.

*Important that steak be of uniform shape and thickness about 1 inch or cooking times will vary.

GRILLED STEAK SOUTHWESTERN

½ c. wine vinegar
½ c. brown sugar, firmly packed
¼ c. catsup
¼ c. soy sauce
2 Tbsp. Worcestershire sauce

1 tsp. prepared mustard
½ tsp. garlic salt
1 tsp. coarsely ground pepper
3 lbs. beef top round steak or
    sirloin, preferred

Glaze:

¾ c. sour cream　　　　　　　　　**1 tsp. green onion, chopped**
2 tsp. prepared horseradish

Mix first seven ingredients for marinade. Sprinkle both sides of steak with pepper and rub in with palm of hand. Place steak in marinade and cover. Refrigerate for 24 hours, turning several times. (If using top round, pierce meat.) This meat may be cooked on grill ... five inches above coals to desired doneness (about 15 min. per side, brushing occasionally with marinade) or may be cut into several uniform pieces, placed on a rack in circle fashion, or individually and cooked at 100% power 6 min. per lb. for well done, 5 min. per pound for medium and 4 min. per pound for rare. When meat is microwaved, this large amount of meat must be divided, cooking 1 - 1½ lbs. each time and not all at once to insure even cooking. Combine glaze ingredients and spread on steak. Cook steak an additional 30 seconds at 100% power. To serve, slice thinly across grain. 6 - 8 servings.

BEEF TENDERLOIN

4 - 5 lb. tenderloin, peeled (2 - 3　　**Savor**
**　　lb. when trimmed)**　　　　　　**Pepper**
Thyme　　　　　　　　　　　　　**Garlic, optional**
Paprika　　　　　　　　　　　　**Browning powder**
Basil

Fold thin tip of tenderloin under and secure with string or rubber bands to form uniform shape. Season tenderloin with spices, pressing into meat on all sides. Shield ends with aluminum foil to prevent overcooking. Place on meat rack. Estimate cooking time as follows: Well done = 9 min. per lb. at 70% power, medium = 8 - 8½ min. per pound at 70%, rare = 7 - 7½ min. per pound at 70%. If cooking with probe internal temperature should be: Rare 120 degrees; med. rare 125 degrees, medium 135 degrees, medium well 140 degrees, well 145 degrees. Standing time causes internal heat to raise 10 - 15 degrees. Cook for ½ of cooking time and turn over. Finish cooking, but remove aluminum shielding for the last ⅓ cooking time. Tent meat with aluminum foil, shiny side in allow to stand 10 - 15 min. to finish cooking. (Some people like to cook first couple of minutes at 100% power to "sear." May wish to try both methods.) Please refer to MEAT CHART for additional information on cooking meats and temperature.

BRISKET

3 - 5 lb. brisket (after being well
    trimmed)*
Coarse black pepper
⅔ c. soy sauce
½ c. vinegar
1 tsp. paprika
1 Tbsp. catsup

1 tsp. garlic powder
1 tsp. onion powder
1 Tbsp. Worcestershire sauce
1 tsp. browning powder
1 Tbsp. liquid smoke, optional
1 c. barbecue sauce

Pierce meat after trimming well and press pepper into meat. Mix next 7 ingredients and pour over meat. Marinate overnight. (Add liquid smoke, if desired.) When ready to cook sprinkle with browning powder and starting with thickest end of meat, roll brisket and tie or rubber band to hold loaf shape, or meat may be cut into two uniform pieces and placed end to end to form a uniform piece if you do not wish to roll. Place in browning bag along with at least ½ of marinade (all should be used for larger brisket), close end with plastic strip, leaving closing loose so steam can partially escape. Place in roasting pan. Cook at 100% power until liquid is hot. Reduce heat and cook 25-30% power or 20-25 minutes per pound. Turn brisket over several times during cooking. Discard juices after ¾ cooking time has passed and add barbecue sauce. Finish cooking the last ¼ of cooking time and then allow meat to stand 10-15 minutes before removing from bag. (Remember juices make wonderful gravy.)

*You may use same instructions and use a 7 - 8 lb. trimmed brisket, but use all of marinade when cooking. Smaller roasts seem to be more tender, however.

LAZY DAY POT ROAST

3 - 4 lb. chuck roast
4 - 6 cloves garlic
½ tsp. Italian spices
Dash of cayenne pepper
1 onion, sliced into rings

½ c. sherry or wine
1½ c. beef bouillon
Carrots and potatoes, optional
1 - 2 Tbsp. flour

At even intervals, pierce meat and insert garlic cloves or halved garlic cloves on front and back side of meat. Sprinkle with spices. Add wine and remaining ingredients along with roast into browning bag that has been coated with flour. Tie bag loosely so some steam may escape. Cook for 8 - 10 minutes at 100% power until liquid is very hot and simmering. Lower heat to 20 - 30% power and slow cook for 1½ - 2½ hours until meat and vegetables are very tender. Turn meat over at least once.

IMPOSSIBLE CHEESEBURGER PIE

1 lb. ground beef	3 eggs
1 med. onion, chopped	¾ c. buttermilk baking mix
½ tsp. seasoning salt	2 tomatoes, sliced
¼ tsp. pepper	1 c. (4 oz.) shredded Cheddar
1 tsp. prepared mustard	cheese
1¼ c. milk	Paprika

Crumble ground beef with onion into a cook/drain container. Microwave, uncovered for 5 - 6 minutes at 100% power. Stir once to separate meat into small pieces. Mix in salt, pepper and mustard. Set aside. Combine milk, baking mix and eggs in blender or mixing bowl. Process 15 seconds or beat with hand beater until smooth. Place hamburger in 9" pie plate. Pour egg mixture over hamburger. Microwave, uncovered for 6 minutes at 100% power until edge is set, rotating once if necessary. Microwave an additional 4 - 5 minutes at 50% power, uncovered until center is set. Top with tomato slices and cheese. Sprinkle with paprika. Microwave, uncovered for 1½ - 2 minutes at 100% power until cheese is melted. Let stand for 10 minutes before serving. Cut into wedges.

CHILI WEEKEND CONCOCTION

1½ - 2 lb. ground beef	1 can (10¾ oz.) mushroom soup
1 onion, chopped	1½ - 2 c. grated Cheddar cheese
1 can (10 oz.) tomatoes and	1 pkg. (12 oz.) corn chips
chilies	1 tsp. chili powder (optional)
2 cans (15½ oz.) chili beans in	
gravy	

In cook/drain container cook beef and onion for 7 - 9 minutes, uncovered at 100% power. Add tomatoes, soup and beans and simmer for 3 - 5 minutes at 100% power, uncovered. In 2 - 3 quart casserole or in individual casseroles layer bean/soup mixture, cheese and chips. Repeat, ending with chips. Cook uncovered for 8 - 10 minutes at 50% power.

EGGPLANT MOUSSAKA

1 (1 lb.) eggplant, peeled and cut	¼ tsp. pepper
into ½" cubes	¾ c. grated Parmesan cheese
1 tsp. butter	Bechamel Sauce*
¼ tsp. salt	¼ tsp. basil, oregano, cinnamon
1 lb. lean ground beef	1 (8 oz.) can tomato sauce
⅓ c. chopped onion	¼ c. grated Cheddar cheese
1 garlic clove, minced	1 Tbsp. crumbs
½ tsp. salt	

Microwave the eggplant and butter, covered for 5 minutes at 100% power. Drain and sprinkle lightly with salt. Recover and set aside. In drain/cook container, cook meat and onion, covered with wax paper for 2 minutes at 100% power. Stir and cook another 2 - 3 minutes. Add salt, seasonings and tomato sauce after cooking. Prepare sauce *(see Bechamel Sauce recipe). Place a layer of eggplant in bottom of 1½ qt. dish. Place all of meat on top. Add another layer of eggplant and then pour sauce over casserole. Sprinkle with grated cheese and crumbs. Microwave uncovered for 4 minutes at 100% power.

REUBEN IN A CASSEROLE

1 can (16 oz.) sauerkraut, rinsed and drained well
1 can (12 oz.) corned beef or 12 oz. corned beef, cooked and chopped
2½ c. shredded Swiss cheese
⅔ c. mayonnaise

⅓ c. Thousand Island salad dressing
2 med. tomatoes, peeled and thinly sliced
⅓ c. rye bread crumbs, toasted
2 Tbsp. butter, melted

Arrange sauerkraut in bottom of 1½ qt. glass or ceramic dish. Layer corned beef and cheese over sauerkraut. Combine mayonnaise and salad dressing. Spread over cheese. Cover with tomato slices. Toss bread crumbs in melted butter and sprinkle over the top. Cook at 50 - 70% power until heated through, approximately 13 - 17 minutes, uncovered. Serve immediately.

ELEGANT STEAK AND RICE

1½ lb. boneless beef round steak, tenderized
2 large onions, cut in ½" slices and separated into rings
1 can (4 oz.) sliced mushrooms drained (reserving liquid)

1 can (10¾ oz.) condensed cream of mushroom soup
½ c. dry sherry
1¼ tsp. garlic salt
3 c. hot cooked rice

Cut steaks into thin strips. Sprinkle with browning and place in with onions in single layer in flat pan. Cook for 2 - 3 minutes, covered at 100% power until meat and onions partially cook. Blend in soup, sherry and ⅔ of mushroom liquid. Add mushrooms, cover with plastic wrap and cook for 15 minutes at 50% power; add garlic salt and continue to cook at 10 - 30% for an additional 30 minutes or until meat is tender. Serve over bed of fluffy rice.

STUFFED PEPPERS

1 lb. ground beef
¾ c. chopped onion
½ Tbsp. olive oil, optional
1 clove garlic, minced
⅓ c. chili sauce
¼ pkg. onion soup mix
¼ pkg. brown gravy mix

½ tsp. salt
1¼ c. min. rice
1 can (8 oz.) tomato sauce
½ tsp. basil
⅛ tsp. pepper
4 large green peppers
⅓ c. grated Cheddar cheese

Combine onion, garlic and oil. Cook for 1 - 1½ minute, uncovered 100% power. Crumble ground beef into onion mixture and cook for 3 - 4 minutes, stirring once at 100% power. Drain off excess fat. Stir in chili sauce, onion and gravy mix and salt. Cook an additional 1 - 2 minutes at 100% power. Stir in rice, tomato sauce and spices. Prepare peppers, removing tops and pulps. Fill each with ¼ of mixture and place in baking dish or cup cake baker. Cover with plastic wrap and cook for 10 - 15 minutes at 100% power until peppers are tender. Top with cheese during the last minute. Let stand 2 - 3 minutes before serving.

LAMB

LEG OF LAMB

1 leg of lamb	Pepper
Garlic cloves	Paprika
Basil	Browning powder, optional
Thyme	

Rub leg with spices and tuck garlic buds into small holes made with sharp knife. Shield small end with aluminum foil and place meat on roasting rack. Cook as follows: Well done 9 min. per lb. at 70% power, medium done 8 - 8½ min. per lb. at 70% power, rare 7 - 7½ min. per lb. at 70% power. If this is a large leg, turn over half way through cooking time. Unshield for the last ⅓ to ¼ of cooking time. Also, if you like a more moist roast, cover lightly with wax paper during cooking. Allow meat to stand for a least 10 - 15 min., tented with aluminum foil, shiny side in to finish cooking. If cooking with probe, remember rare is 120 degrees, medium 135 degrees and well 145 degrees as it cooks during standing time. (Refer to MEAT CHART for additional information on meat.)

PORK

SAUSAGE STUFFED EGGPLANT

¼ c. dry bread crumbs
¾ lb. pork sausage
1 med. eggplant
½ c. chopped onion
1 can (4 oz.) mushrooms,
   drained
1 tsp. Worcestershire sauce

½ tsp. seasoning salt
¼ tsp. basil
¼ tsp. thyme
¼ tsp. Greek seasoning
¾ c. shredded Cheddar cheese
Parsley

Break up sausage and place in drainer/cooker. Cook for 3½ - 4 minutes at 100% power. While sausage cooks, cut eggplant in half and scoop out the centers. Coarsely chop and cook eggplant with chopped onion for 3 - 4 minutes, covered at 100% power. Stir in mushrooms, crumbs, seasonings and sausage. Stuff eggplant and microwave covered at 100% power for 5 - 6 minutes. Sprinkle with cheese and cook uncovered at 50% power for 1½ - 2 minutes until cheese melts.

ZUCCHINI MEAT BOATS

4 - 8" to 10" zucchini (1½ to 2
   lbs.)
2 Tbsp. margarine
½ c. chopped green onions
2 Tbsp. parsley
¾ tsp. dried Italian herbs
¼ tsp. ground white pepper

1 c. fresh whole wheat bread
   crumbs, grated (about 2½
   slices)
½ tsp. garlic salt
1 lb. cheese hot dogs
8 cherry tomatoes, split (opt.)

Cut ends off zucchini and split in half lengthwise. Scoop out each half to make boats with sides ¼ to ½ inch thick. Chop scooped out zucchini and onions. Mix with spices and cook for 2 - 4 minutes at 100% power, covered, until zucchini is just tender. Add bread crumbs and mix well. Stuff zucchini with mixture and top with hot dog chunks and cook at 100% power, covered, approximately 6 minutes per pound. Garnish with tomatoes during standing time.

GLAZED HAM

1 (3 to 4 lb.) precooked ham
¼ c. currant jelly (or your
   favorite jelly)

1 tsp. allspice
½ tsp. ginger
1 Tbsp. brown sugar

Score ham and place on roasting rack. Mix jelly, spices and sugar in small bowl. Heat for 1 minute at 50% power to blend spices. Baste ham on all sides. Cover with waxed paper and cook for 6 minutes per pound at 50% power. Turn ham over rotissiere style, a quarter of the way each fourth of cooking time, basting after each turn. Decorate, if desired with pineapple, fruit, etc. during last fourth of cooking period and cook uncovered for the last fourth of cooking. Allow to stand 15 - 20 minutes before serving. Ham may be shielded during last half of cooking time to prevent ends from drying if necessary.

HAM AND BROCCOLI CASSEROLE

2 pkgs. (10 oz.) frozen broccoli
   spears
2 c. cubed ham
1 can (3 oz.) French fried onion
   rings

1 c. shredded Cheddar cheese
1 can cream of mushroom soup
¼ c. milk
½ tsp. Greek seasoning or
   favorite spice

     Place vegetables in microwave and defrost at 50% power for 4 - 6 min. Drain well and arrange broccoli flowerettes toward center in round baking dish. Top with ham and one-half of onion rings. Sprinkle with cheese. Blend soup and milk with spice. Pour over casserole. Microwave covered with wax paper for 8 - 10 minutes at 100% power. Sprinkle with remaining onion rings and microwave uncovered for 5 - 6 minutes at 100% power until heated through.

BAR B Q RIBS WITH SAUERKRAUT

2½ - 3 lbs. spare ribs, cut into 3"
   sections*
1 onion, thinly sliced
½ tsp. basil
1 onion, chopped
1 apple, finely chopped
1 (1 - 1½ lb.) can sauerkraut,
   drained

1 tsp. lemon juice
2 Tbsp. brown sugar
1 tsp. caraway seed
Small amount barbecue sauce
   and browning sauce

     Arrange ribs *(country style ribs may be used) around side of baking dish, meatiest portions to outside. Spread with onion rings and sprinkle with basil. Cover with waxed paper and cook for 5 minutes at 100% power. Reduce heat to 50% power and continue to cook for 13 minutes. Rearrange half way through cooking time for even cooking. Drain ribs and remove. Mix sauerkraut, onion, apple, lemon, brown sugar and caraway seed. Place in baking dish. Brush ribs with browning/barbeque sauce mixture, cover with waxed paper and cook for 15 - 20 minutes at 50% power. Brush ribs again and cook, uncovered for 5 additional minutes at 50% power.

SAVORY PORK CHOPS

1 - 2 Tbsp. oil
2 heaping tsp. minced garlic
1 Tbsp. finely chopped almonds,
   optional
1 Tbsp. golden raisins, optional
2 heaping tsp. dried Mexican
   oregano, crumbled
3 bay leaves
½ tsp. sugar

½ tsp. salt
⅓ tsp. freshly ground pepper
1 med. onion, sliced
1½ c. fresh orange juice
½ c. water
6¾ inch thick pork chops
¼ c. water
2 tsp. cornstarch
2 - 3 oz. green chilies, 6 strips

Combine oil and garlic and cook for 20 - 30 seconds at 70% power. Add almonds, raisins and spices. Cook another 20 - 30 seconds. Stir in onion and continue to cook about 1 - 1½ min., covered at 70 - 100% power. Add juice and first amount (½ cup) water. Bring to boil and reduce heat to 50% and cook or simmer about 1 min. Slowly stir ¼ c. water and cornstarch in small bowl. Blend into sauce and cook at about 70% power, stirring once for about 2 - 3 minutes. Reduce heat and simmer additional minute. Spread ½ - ⅓ c. sauce over bottom of large roasting pan. Salt and pepper both sides of pork chops and arrange in dish, meatiest portion to outside of pan. Place 1 strip of green chili on each chop along with 1 Tbsp. of sauce. Cover tightly and bake at 50% power for 11 min. per pound (approximately 20 - 25 min.), rearranging half way through cooking time for even cooking. Reduce heat to very low and continue to cook for another 10 min. or so until chops very tender, but not over done and dry. Let stand a couple of minutes before serving.

PORK CHOPS WITH APPLE DRESSING

⅓ c. each chopped celery,
   carrot and onion
1 Tbsp. butter, optional
¼ tsp. ground sage
Salt and pepper to taste
Dash ground cinnamon
3 c. dressing mix

1½ c. chopped Golden Delicious
   apples (preferred)
⅓ c. walnuts or pecans,
   chopped
¼ c. raisins
½ - ⅔ c. chicken broth
4 pork chops (4 - 6 oz. each)

Combine celery, carrot and onion with butter in 8 cup measure. Cover with plastic wrap and cook for 1 - 1½ min. at 100% power. Combine vegetable mixture with dressing mix, apples, nuts and raisins. Add enough chicken broth to moisten mixture. Place dressing in bottom of 2 quart shallow oblong casserole dish. Arrange pork chops in single layer over dressing, placing thickest part of chops to outside of casserole. Sprinkle with pepper.* Cook 9 minutes per pound (weigh dish, then fill dish to determine weight) at 70% power, covered with waxed paper. *May also sprinkle with browning powder. Salt during standing time. Rearrange pork chops half way through cooking time if necessary, but do not turn over.

PORK CHOPS AVEC ONION

4 pork chops, cut 1" thick
¼ c. seasoned bread crumbs
1 Tbsp. oil
½ tsp. salt

½ tsp. Greek seasoning, opt.
¼ tsp. pepper
2 med. onions, thinly sliced

Place seasoned bread crumbs on waxed paper. Press meat into crumbs, coating well on both sides. Set aside. Preheat browning skillet at 100% power for 5 minutes. Add oil and tilt dish to coat. Place chops in dish and cook, uncovered for 1 minute at 100% power. Turn chops and cook for an additional minute. Arrange chops with the thickest part to the outside of dish. Season and spread onion slices over the top of chops. Cover, reduce power to 50% and cook for 10 - 12 minutes. Turn chops, replace onion rings and continue to cook an additional 10 - 15 minutes until meat loses its pink next to the bone.

PORK CHOPS WITH PEAS AND CREAMY RICE

1 can (10¾ oz.) cream of
    mushroom soup
½ c. sour cream
½ tsp. salt
¼ tsp. ginger
¼ tsp. rosemary leaves,
    crushed
½ c. shredded Cheddar cheese

1 pkg. (10 oz.) frozen peas
1 can (4 oz.) mushroom stems
    and pieces, drained
1 can (3 oz.) French fried onion
    rings, divided
½ c. instant rice
4 - 5 pork chops, ½ - ¾" thick

In medium bowl blend soup, cream and seasonings. In a 12 x 8" dish combine ¾ of soup mixture with peas, mushrooms, cheese, half of onion rings and rice.

Arrange pork chops on top of rice mixture, meatiest portion to outside of dish. Spoon remaining sauce over chops. (Meat may first be sprinkled with browning powder, if available.) Cover with wax paper and microwave at 100% power for 10 minutes. Rotate dish and reduce power to 50% for 12 - 17 minutes, depending on number of chops and their thickness.* Uncover, sprinkle with onions and increase power. Cook at 100% power for 3 - 4 minutes to finish cooking. Let stand for a few minutes before serving.

*(If chops are very thick, you may want to turn over during second cooking period.)

PORK CHOPS WITH SAUERKRAUT AND BEER

4 pork chops, 1 inch thick
1 can (16 oz.) sauerkraut,
    drained

1 tsp. caraway seed
½ c. chopped onion
1 can (12 oz.) beer

Arrange pork chops in 8 inch baking dish with thick part to outside and ends to middle. Sprinkle with onion, then top with kraut. Sprinkle with caraway seed and pour beer around the chops. Cover tightly and microwave at 50% power for 35 - 40 minutes. Rotate dish once during cooking time and allow to stand a few minutes before serving.

PORK STUFFED TURNIPS

6 med. turnips (2½ - 3 lbs.)
½ tsp. sugar
4 slices bacon
1 lb. lean diced pork
½ lb. fresh mushrooms,
    quartered

2 tsp. Greek seasoning
½ tsp. white pepper
1 can (8½ oz.) small sweet peas,
    drained
Seasoned bread crumbs

Peel turnips and slice off bottom so each turnip will stand up straight. Sprinkle with sugar. Cover tightly and microwave for 6 minutes per pound at 100% power. After cooling, use melon baller or spoon and remove center, leaving a ¼ inch shell. Reserve cores. Drain dish and return turnips to plate. Place in circle fashion. Microwave bacon for 4 minutes at 100% power, until crisp, reserving fat. Crumble bacon and set aside. In remaining fat saute diced pork, chopped turnip cores and mushrooms at 100% power for 6 minutes. Drain. Add seasonings and peas and toss lightly. Stuff turnip shells and sprinkle with crumbled bacon and crumbs. Place extra stuffing in center of turnips and cook all for 6 minutes at 100% power, uncovered.

ROAST LOIN OF PORK WITH APRICOT GLAZE

1 c. dried apricots, coarsely
    chopped
¾ c. orange juice
½ c. apricot nectar
Juice and peel of ½ of med.
    lemon, seeds removed

1 Tbsp. honey
¼ tsp. ground cinnamon and
    allspice
3½ lb. boneless pork loin roast

Mix all ingredients, except pork in a 4 cup measure. Microwave for 8 - 10 minutes, uncovered at 100% power or until apricots are restored and tender. Stir once or twice, if needed. Discard lemon peel and set aside. In a cooking bag* which has been punctured, place pork on roasting rack. Shield both ends of roast with strips of aluminum foil to prevent overcooking and top with half of glaze. Microwave for 5 minutes at 100% power. Reduce power to 70% power and microwave for 25 - 40 minutes, removing the foil after 15 minutes.

Internal temperature should be 160 degrees. Remove from oven and cover loosely with foil until internal temperature is 170 degrees (about 15 minutes). Spoon remaining sauce over roast and serve. *Cooking bags give more even heat for pork cookery in the microwave. Also won't be necessary to baste as self-basting takes place. Place pork on rack and pan. Place entire pan in bag - you will find it easier to handle throughout cooking.

FRUITED PORK ROAST

¾ c. brown sugar
¾ c. dried fruit
¾ c. hot water
¼ c. plus 2 Tbsp. concentrated
    frozen orange juice, divided
    and defrosted
1 small onion, sliced

½ tsp. ginger
¼ tsp. salt
⅛ tsp. pepper
¼ tsp. marjoram
1 Tbsp. butter
3 lb. boneless pork loin roast

    In 1 quart combine ½ c. brown sugar, fruit, water and ¼ c. orange concentrate, ginger, etc. Microwave 100% power for 8 - 12 minutes until fruit is softened, stir occasionally. Set aside. Melt butter in small bowl for 30 - 45 seconds at 100% power. Stir in remaining sugar and 2 Tbsp. orange concentrate. Place roast in bag, fat side down, on roasting rack.* Spread with butter mixture. Cook 7 minutes 100% power. Reduce to 50% power and cook 8 minutes. Turn roast and insert meat thermometer. Spoon half of sauce over top. Microwave at 50% power for 15 - 18 minutes or until internal temperature reaches 165 degrees. Spoon on remaining sauce and let stand tented with aluminum for 10 minutes or until internal temperature reaches 170 degrees. Be sure to check in several spots for uniform temperature. *I cook pork roasts in cooking bags as even heat is very important to pork cookery. You may puncture bag after roast is turned. This will allow some juices to drain which is necessary for tender meats, or place entire pan and roasting rack in bag. This makes easy handling - just slip it in and out of bag as needed.

POULTRY

CHICKEN MEAL IN A DISH VARIATION

½ c. rice, cooked
½ boneless chicken breast
Fresh spinach or ½ c. frozen
   spinach, defrosted
Chutney or topping such as jelly

Green pepper and onion rings
Fruit slice (cantaloupe,
   pineapple, etc.)
Spice (thyme, basil, pepper,
   paprika, etc.) at least two

Place layer of rice in bottom of individual au gratin dish. Top with spinach or vegetable of your choice. Top with chicken breast. Brush chicken with chutney or jelly. Top with green pepper/onion rings and sprinkle with spices. Place fruit slice on top of this and cover with plastic wrap. Microwave for 3 - 4 minutes at 100% power. If salt is used, salt during standing time. Any combination of your favorite foods can be used in this manner.

FRIED CHICKEN

1 envelope (4¼ oz.) crispy
   crumb coating for chicken
¾ c. whole wheat flake cereal,
   crushed
1 Tbsp. dried parsley flakes

½ tsp. salt
¼ c. butter or margarine
1 egg
1½ Tbsp. milk
4 - 4½ lbs. chicken parts

Mix crumb coating, cereal, parsley and salt in shallow dish and set aside. Place butter pie plate and microwave at 100% power for 45 seconds to 1 min. until melted. Beat in eggs and milk. Dip the chicken into egg mixture, then into crumb/cereal mixture, pressing firmly to coat. Place ½ of chicken, bone side down on roasting rack with meatiest parts toward the outside. Microwave for 6-6½ minutes per pound at 100% power. (May cover with paper towel to prevent splattering if you wish.) * Rearrange half way through cooking time so less cooked parts are towards the outside. DO NOT TURN OVER. Repeat with remainder of chicken. Let stand a while before serving. If you wish to serve cold, refrigerate uncovered until cool and then wrap or put in container. *Since this chicken is cooked uncovered, the "no cover" lid is used if any at all.

FABULOUS CHICKEN CASSEROLE

1 c. diced cooked ham
1 large chicken (4 - 5 lb.)
1 (3 oz.) can mushrooms,
  reserving liquid
1 c. ripe olives, sliced and
  reserving liquid
6 c. cooked frozen noodles (¾
  lb.)
⅓ c. minced onion
⅓ c. minced green pepper

1 can condensed cream of
  mushroom soup
1½ c. (⅓ lb.) grated processed
  cheese
¼ c. minced pimentos
1 c. frozen peas, thawed
⅓ tsp. pepper
½ tsp. salt
½ tsp. celery salt

Add 1 Tbsp. salt, celery tops, 1 slice onion, 1 bay leaf and stew chicken in microwave according to directions or conventionally. Remove from broth, chill then chunk chicken and chill the broth. Skim the fat from broth and re-serve. To broth add the mushroom and olive juices. To this add enough water to make 6 cups of liquid, bring to boil and cook noodles until tender. While the noodles are cooking, take 2 Tbsp. of chicken fat and saute or cook the onions, peppers and mushrooms for 1 - 2 minutes at 100% power. Add vegetables to the chicken with half of the olives. To the drained noodles add soup and the next six ingredients. In a 3 quart casserole arrange the noodles and chicken in layers, ending with the noodles. Top with the ham and the rest of the olives. Chill so flavors will mix. Bake at 50% power for 25 - 30 minutes uncovered until bubbly. You can put this casserole into two smaller casseroles, cooking one for 12 - 15 minutes and freezing the other for a later time. Don't forget when you freeze casseroles, freeze in pan until solid, then pop out of pan, wrap in freezer paper with directions for cooking and date of freezing on package for later use. This puts your pan back in circulation and you won't have to guess how to cook it when you get ready to pop it back in the original pan to cook it.

CHICKEN CHASSEUR

1 lb. boneless chicken breast,
  skinned and cut into strips
⅓ c. cornstarch
¼ c. vegetable oil, optional
½ tsp. each, tarragon and
  ground thyme
¼ tsp. pepper

1 c. sliced scallions
1¾ c. chicken broth
¾ c. cooking sherry
1 c. sliced mushrooms
3 tomatoes, cut into eighths
3 - 4 c. hot cooked rice

Dredge chicken in cornstarch. Place in serving dish and cook, uncov-ered, at 100% power for 2 - 3 minutes rearranging for even cooking. Stir in sea-sonings and scallions. Cook 1 more minute. Add oil and remaining cornstarch. Mix well with broth and sherry. Cover and cook mixture at 70% power for 3 - 4 minutes. Gently stir in mushrooms and tomatoes, cover and simmer an additional 2 - 3 minutes. Serve over rice or pass sauce separately. Notice the similar cooking techniques. Microwave vs. conventional. Searing chicken, etc., then lowering heat as you would in conventional methods.

CHICKEN DIJONNAIS

½ c. oil
¼ c. fresh lemon
½ tsp. freshly ground pepper
6 (8 oz.) chicken breasts,
   skinned and boned
3 Tbsp. tarragon vinegar
2 Tbsp. dry white wine
1 tsp. tarragon

½ tsp. white pepper
12 Tbsp. butter
Paprika, optional
Browning powder, optional
2 Tbsp. Dijon mustard
Lemon slices and parsley sprigs
   (garnish)

Combine oil, lemon juice and pepper in shallow dish. Swirl chicken in mixture and allow to marinate, covered in refrigerator for at least 30 minutes. Combine vinegar and wine in 2 cup measure. Bring to a boil at 100% power and continue to boil until liquid is reduced to about 2 Tbsp. Remove and add tarragon and pepper. Whisk in butter, one tablespoon at a time, blending thoroughly after each addition. Heat at 50% power and continue whisking in butter additions until sauce is slightly thickened. Add mustard, set aside, but keep warm.

Place chicken breasts on rack, meaty parts to outside. Sprinkle with paprika and/or browning powder. Cook for 6 - 6½ minutes per pound. Rearrange half way through cooking time and baste lightly, both sides with sauce. Allow chicken to stand for a few minutes to finish cooking, basting at this time. Serve extra sauce along side chicken when serving.

*Leave center of rack empty if you do not wish to bother with rearranging - this is called "circle fashion."

CHICKEN STUFFED WITH ASPARAGUS

2 chicken breasts, boned and
   split in half
¾ lb. fresh asparagus, cut into 1
   inch pieces
Browning powder

½ c. salad dressing
4 Tbsp. milk
2 Tbsp. lemon juice
1 tsp. tarragon leaves
½ tsp. basil

Place each piece of breast between plastic wrap and pound with flat meat mallet. Set aside. Cook asparagus for 2½ - 3 minutes, covered at 100% power. Allow to cool after draining. Place ⅛ of asparagus on each piece of chicken and roll up.* Sprinkle with browning powder and cook on meat rack covered with waxed paper for 8 - 12 minutes. Combine salad dressing, milk, lemon juice and spices. Spoon over chicken and microwave uncovered for 1 - 2 minutes at 100% power until heated through. *Freeze half of chicken for later use if desired. Will freeze up to 4 months. If you freeze half, cut sauce ingredients by half, too. Also cook chicken 4 - 6 minutes for ½ of recipe.

CHICKEN BREASTS STUFFED WITH CRAB MEAT

1 can (5 oz.) crab meat, rinsed
   drained and flaked (or
   equivalent in fresh meat)
¼ c. chopped green onion
2 eggs
1 Tbsp. parsley flakes

2 tsp. lemon juice
¼ tsp. pepper
2 chicken breasts, boned,
   skinned and halved
⅓ - ½ c. seasoned bread
   crumbs

Lightly pound chicken breasts to flatten slightly. The easy way to do this is with the bottom of a pan so you won't pierce the meat. In a small mixing bowl combine crab meat, onion, spices and 1 egg. Place one-fourth of the mixture on each breast and spread evenly. Roll up the breast like a jelly roll. Dip each breast into the other egg, which has been beaten and roll in the crumbs to coat evenly. Place the rolls seam side down in 9 inch round pie plate or dish. Place them in as much "circle fashion" as possible leaving even distance between each and nothing in center. This will help them cook more evenly. Cover with waxed paper, the "crack the lid" cover so that some steam can escape and some will remain for a partial steaming effect. Microwave for 6½ - 9½ minutes (6 minutes per pound). Let stand for a few minutes so chicken will finish cooking.

CHICKEN WITH SHERRIED CHEESE SAUCE

4 Tbsp. butter
1 c. Italian bread crumbs
2 Tbsp. grated Parmesan
   cheese
1 Tbsp. dried parsley flakes
1 tsp. paprika

4 large whole boned chicken
   breasts, split and skin
   removed
Dash nutmeg
Sliced black olives
Slivered almonds, optional

Sauce:

2 Tbsp. butter
2 Tbsp. flour
½ tsp. salt
Dash pepper
¼ tsp. seasoning salt or favorite
   spice

1¼ c. milk
2 Tbsp. sherry
1 c. Swiss cheese, shredded

Place ¼ cup butter in 9" pie plate. Microwave for 45 - 60 seconds at 100% power until melted. In another pie plate mix bread crumbs, Parmesan, parsley and paprika. Dip each piece of chicken in butter and coat with crumb mixture. Place on rack and microwave at 100% power for 10 - 14 minutes or until mixture runs clear. Rearrange half way through according to size and shape. Let stand covered (cover according to texture wanted: Paper towel - crusty, wax - medium dry, plastic - moist). Place 2 Tbsp. butter in 4 cup measure. Cook at 100% power for 30 - 45 seconds until butter is melted. Stir in flour, salt, pepper, spices, blend in milk and sherry. Microwave for 4 - 5 minutes at 100% power until thickened. Blend in Swiss cheese until cheese melts. Serve over chicken. Garnish with almonds and sliced black olives.

GOURMET CHICKEN BREASTS

6 boneless chicken breasts,
    halved and skinned
1 c. sour cream and chives
2 Tbsp. lemon juice
2 tsp. Worcestershire sauce
½ tsp. celery salt
1 tsp. paprika

¼ tsp. garlic powder
1½ tsp. salt
¼ tsp. cayenne pepper
¾ c. seasoned bread crumbs
¼ c. pecans, chopped
¼ c. margarine

Sauce*:

1 Tbsp. butter, melted
½ c. black raspberry preserves
3 oz. frozen orange juice
    concentrate

2 Tbsp. dry sherry
½ tsp. dry mustard
Dash of ginger, salt and cayenne

Rinse and dry chicken breasts. In 2 quart dish combine sour cream, lemon, Worcestershire and spices. Add chicken, coating each piece well and let stand covered in refrigerator for at least 8 hours or overnight.

When ready to cook carefully remove coated chicken from cream mixture and roll in crumb/nut mixture, coating evenly. Arrange in "circle fashion" in shallow baking dish, thickest portion to outside. Drizzle with butter, cover with paper towel and cook for 6 - 6½ minutes per pound at 100% power. Let stand to finish cooking.

*Mix all sauce ingredients in 2 cup container and heat until well blended or almost boiling, 1 - 2 minutes at 100% power. Pour over chicken and serve.

CHICKEN WITH FRESH MUSHROOM STUFFING

2 c. fresh sliced mushrooms
½ c. chopped onion
½ c. chopped celery
2 Tbsp. butter, optional
½ - ¾ c. chicken broth
3 c. seasoned stuffing mix

1 egg
⅓ c. seasoned bread crumbs
1 tsp. parsley
½ tsp. each paprika and basil
2½ - 3 lb. fryer parts (skin may
    be removed, if desired)

Combine onion and celery with butter (optional), cook 100% power covered for approximately 3 minutes. Add mushrooms and cook an additional minute. (If butter is not used, increase liquids slightly.) Bring chicken broth to boil, approximately 60 seconds at 100% power. Add stuffing mix and egg. Mix well and pat into uniform base over bottom of baking dish. Combine crumbs, spices and ¼ tsp. salt. Coat chicken and place on stuffing, meatiest portion of chicken to outside of pan. Cover with wax paper and cook at 100% power for 10 minutes. Rearrange chicken, but do not turn over. Microwave approximately 7 - 10 minutes longer. Allow chicken to stand to finish cooking.

CHICKEN PARMESAN

2½ lb. chicken, cut up or
   boneless chicken breasts
Cayenne pepper
Onion powder
Garlic powder

½ c. grated Parmesan cheese
2 c. seasoned bread crumbs
2 - 3 eggs, well beaten with 2
   Tbsp. milk
¼ c. butter, melted

Clean chicken and pat dry with paper towels. Season chicken with pepper, onion and garlic powder. Mix the cheese and bread crumbs in flat dish. Place egg mixture in a flat dish. Dip chicken in egg mixture, then into crumb mixture. Place chicken in flat dish, meaty portions towards the outside of the dish. Pour butter over chicken and sprinkle with remaining crumbs. Cover with waxed paper and cook at 100% power for 18 - 25 minutes.* Rotate dish rearranging chicken if necessary. Salt during standing time.

*Boneless meat takes less time, approximately 6 - 7 minutes per pound. The "plus" minutes added per pound here is due to the added ingredients other than the meat, and this must be allowed for. Otherwise, 6 minutes per pound is our "base" per pound for meats.

STUFFED CHICKEN THIGHS

¼ c. chopped onion
¼ c. chopped celery
2 Tbsp. margarine, optional
½ tsp. poultry seasoning
1 c. herbed seasoned stuffing
   mix

⅓ c. chicken bouillon
4 chicken thighs, skin on
1 Tbsp. butter, melted
1 Tbsp. browning sauce

Combine onion, celery with butter (optional) and microwave for 1 minute, covered. Add bouillon and microwave an additional minute at 100% power. Stir in stuffing mix. Lift skin on each thigh and stuff with ¼ of stuffing mix. Pull skin over meat and place on roasting rack, skin side up. Brush with butter and browning sauce and microwave at 100% power, uncovered for 6 - 6½ minutes per pound. Rearrange half way through cooking but do not turn over. Allow meat to stand for a few minutes before serving.

CHICKEN TERIYAKI

2 - 3 lb. boneless chicken
    breasts, halved
½ c. soy sauce
¼ c. sherry or white wine

1 clove garlic, finely chopped
2 Tbsp. brown sugar
1 tsp. ginger

Place chicken in plastic bag and mix the remaining ingredients. Pour marinade over chicken and refrigerate for 4 or 5 hours. Remove the chicken from the bag, reserving the marinade. Place chicken in large baking dish, thickest parts of chicken to the outside. Cover with waxed paper and cook for about 10 minutes at 100% power. Baste chicken and finish cooking for 6 - 8 minutes, uncovered until fork tender. Chicken will cook about 6 minutes a pound "plus" to allow for marinade. Cook ½ time, uncover, baste and check for even cooking. Rearrange if some of the pieces aren't cooking evenly. Arranging chicken in a circle on a round serving dish would eliminate this step. Let stand 5 minutes or so before serving. Always remember to allow standing time for meat to finish cooking. This takes 20% of total cooking time. Water molecules cause friction and heat while bumping together and it takes this long for them to stop after the oven turns off.

CHICKEN ARTICHOKE "DELUXE"

1 c. sour cream
2 Tbsp. fresh chopped parsley
½ tsp. salt
¼ tsp. white pepper
1 Tbsp. lemon juice
8 halves chicken breasts (about
    2 lbs.), boned
2 med. onions, thinly sliced
1 tsp. chicken bouillon granules

1 (4 oz.) can sliced mushrooms,
    drained (reserve ¼ c. liquid)
2 (8½ oz.) cans artichoke hearts,
    drained and sliced
½ tsp. basil
½ tsp. salt
½ tsp. thyme
Dash cayenne pepper

Mix the sour cream, parsley, salt and pepper with the lemon juice in small serving bowl and refrigerate for several hours so flavors will blend.

To prevent rearranging during the cooking, place chicken (about 1 lb. at a time) on roasting rack in "circle fashion" or at least having a "hole" in middle of the rack. If you fill the rack too full and don't leave the "hole", the middle piece won't cook in the same time as the outside pieces since it will only get two way cooking (up and down) instead of four way like the outside pieces (up and down, inside and outside). Cook each pound 4 - 5 minutes (almost done). Cool enough until you can handle pieces to cut into bite size. Add onions and chicken in serving dish. Cover and cook for about 3 - 4 minutes at 100% power. Dissolve bouillon granules in mushroom liquid and stir into chicken/onion mixture. Add the mushrooms and sliced artichoke hearts with the spices. Stir well. Cover and microwave for 3 minutes at 100% power until tender and hot. Remember do not overcook as ingredients are precooked and we only need to get the mixture hot. Let stand covered for 5 minutes. Serve sour cream sauce over each portion.

CHICKEN OR TURKEY ENCHILADAS CASSEROLE

1 lb. ground turkey or chicken
1½ c. onion, peeled, and diced
2 cans (4 oz.) chopped green
    chiles, drained
1 tsp. salt
2 c. sour cream

1 can (10 oz.) mild enchilada
    sauce
12 frozen corn tortillas, thawed
2 c. (8 oz.) Cheddar cheese,
    coarsely grated

Put turkey and onion in cook/drain container and cook for 3 - 5 minutes at 100% power, stirring once, until turkey loses pink color. In bowl combine meat and onion mixture with chiles, salt and sour cream. Heat enchilada sauce in small bowl for about 1 minute at 100% power. Using a 2 qt. casserole, layer tortillas (4) which have been dipped in sauce, spread with half the turkey mixture and sprinkle with ⅓ of the cheese. Repeat with 4 more enchiladas and then cover with remaining 4 tortillas. Pour remaining sauce over this and sprinkle with remaining cheese. Cover and cook for 15 - 20 minutes at 50% power. Turn dish, if necessary half way through cooking time. Let stand 5 minutes before serving.

CHICKEN MONTEREY

Filling:

2 - 3 c. cooked diced chicken
4 oz. cream cheese
4 oz. sour cream
1 tsp. salt

3 whole jalapeno peppers or
    green chilies (chopped and
    seeded)
⅛ tsp. pepper

Sauce*:

½ c. cooking oil
½ c. flour
1⅓ c. chopped onions
2 green chilies, chopped and
    seeded
2 cups chicken broth
12 corn tortillas

½ c. sour cream
1½ tsp. salt
⅛ tsp. pepper
⅛ tsp. basil
½ c. heavy cream
2 c. grated Monterey Jack
    cheese

In mixing bowl combine cream cheese and sour cream. Stir in peppers, chicken and seasonings. Heat tortillas that have been wrapped in damp towel for 45 minutes at 100% power. (May also dip in warm broth, if desired.) Generously spoon filling onto each along with a small amount of sauce* which has previously been made. Roll and place seam side down in greased 8 x 12 inch dish. Pour on remaining sauce, spoon over sour cream and sprinkle with grated cheese. Microwave for 9 - 10 minutes at 70% power, uncovered.

Sauce: Mix oil and flour in 4 cup measure until smooth and cook at 100% power for 5 minutes until it makes light brown color (roux). Stir in onions and chilies and cook for additional 3 minutes, uncovered. Add broth, spices and cream.

TORTILLAS WITH CHICKEN

1 (10 oz.) can tomatoes and
   green chilies, with liquid
½ tsp. salt
½ c. chicken stock or bouillon
1 (10¾ oz.) can cream of
   mushroom soup

12 corn tortillas, broken into
   quarters
2 c. diced, cooked chicken
3 c. (12 oz.) grated Cheddar
   cheese
2 c. finely chopped onion

Combine first four ingredients in a 4 cup measure, blending well and set aside. Grease an 8x12 inch baking dish and place one-third of the tortillas (4), chicken, sauce, onions and cheese into the dish. Repeat twice more ending with the cheese on top. Microwave for 13 - 14 minutes at 70% power, uncovered and let stand for 5 minutes before serving. Because of the large amount of the cheese you don't want to cook this on high. Remember that dairy products are cooked on a slower oven than many other things. This is true on conventional cooking, to keep cheese from stringing, so it is also true in microwave cooking. Don't forget to use the same methods for both types of cooking.

CHICKEN SPAGHETTI

2 c. cooked, diced chicken
1 c. cooked, diced ham
3 Tbsp. butter
½ c. chopped onion
½ c. chopped green peppers
1 (16 oz.) can stewed tomatoes,
   including liquid
1 tsp. salt

¼ tsp. pepper
¼ tsp. Greek seasoning,
   optional
2½ c. (10 oz.) processed cheese
   (2 c. cubed and ½ c. grated)
1 (8 oz.) pkg. thin spaghetti,
   broken and cooked

Melt butter in 2 quart container for 1 minute at 100% power. Add onion and pepper and cook for 3 minutes at 100% power. Add the tomatoes and spices. Cover and cook another 3 minutes at 100% power. Add cooked spaghetti, chicken, ham and cubed cheese. Cover and cook for 8 minutes at 70% power. Sprinkle with grated cheese and let sit covered until cheese melts.

ROAST TURKEY

1 (10 - 13 lb.) turkey   Stuffing (optional)
1 Tbsp. salt

Basting Sauce:

3 Tbsp. butter   8 drops browning sauce
½ tsp. paprika

Rinse turkey with cold water and pat dry. Salt the cavity and if desired, stuff at this time. Brush with basting sauce made by combining paprika, butter and browning. Shield wings and boney parts with aluminum foil at this time and place breast side down on a roasting rack. A cooking bag is an excellent method to cook this turkey. Punch a couple of holes in bag before placing on the roasting rack so juice will drain. Remove the juice throughout the cooking time. This shortens the time as the microwave doesn't know whether it is cooking the water within the meat or in the pan. Therefore, remove the unneeded liquid. If a cooking bag is not used, cover with waxed paper. Microwave at 70% power for 9 minutes per pound.

Divide cooking time into four equal parts and rotate bird, rotisserie style at the end of each quarter cooking time, removing shields for second half of cooking time. Breast is up for last quarter of cooking time and turkey should be basted each time it is turned. Tent with foil and allow bird to stand an additional 25 - 30 minutes before serving. Standing time is very important to finish cooking the turkey. Test for doneness with meat thermometer (in several spots), 155 degrees will go to 165 degrees during tenting and standing.

TURKEY ROLL UP

1 whole turkey breast   ½ tsp. basil
6 c. of prepared stuffing (your   1 box frozen chopped spinach,
    favorite)   thawed and drained
Salt   1 small pkg. slivered almonds
Pepper

Split whole, boned and thawed breast in half. Skin each half, but reserve skin. Butterfly each piece by cutting horizontally in half, but not through. Open up meat along hinge and pound (covered with plastic wrap) until ½ inch thick. Mix stuffing, spinach and almonds and spread about 3 cups on each half of flattened breast. Roll each breast up, jelly roll style, replace or lay skin on top of each roll and tie securely with string. Brush with butter, sprinkle with spices and cook on rack, 70% power for 9 minutes per pound. Remember, one roll-up may be frozen and reserved for another time.

Don't forget standing time so the turkey will finish cooking, 20 - 25% of total cooking time is necessary standing time to allow all meat to finish cooking. Cook to 80% done so you won't overcook. The rest of the cooking takes place during standing time, whether you want it to or not. Therefore, this time must be allowed for so meats will not overcook. Temperature will raise 10 - 15 degrees during standing.

TURKEY ENCHILADAS

1½ c. coarsely chopped cooked
    turkey
½ c. chopped onions
2½ c. grated Cheddar cheese
2 jalapeno peppers, fresh or
    canned, seeded and
    chopped*

12 soft corn tortillas
1½ c. chicken broth

Wrap the tortillas in a damp cloth and microwave at 100% power for 45 seconds, or dip each tortilla into hot broth. Combine turkey, onion, cheese and peppers. Place a small amount of combined ingredients with 1 Tbsp. broth on each tortilla. Roll and place seam side down in an 8 x 12 inch baking dish. Sprinkle remaining cheese mixture over top of enchiladas and add enough broth to keep enchiladas moist. Cover loosely with waxed paper. Microwave for 6 - 8 minutes at 70% power until cheese is melted and enchiladas are heated through. Serve with picante sauce.

*Chicken can be substituted for turkey and green chilies can be substituted for jalapeno peppers if desired.

VEAL

VEAL PARMIGIANA

1 egg, slightly beaten
2 Tbsp. corn flake crumbs
⅓ c. grated Parmesan cheese
1 lb. veal cutlets or boneless
    round steak*
1 med. onion, chopped

4 oz. (1 cup) Mozzarella cheese,
    sliced or shredded
1 c. (8 oz.) can tomato sauce
Pepper
½ tsp. Italian seasoning
Parmesan cheese

Cook onion for about 1 - 1½ minute at 100% power until partially cooked. In shallow dish beat egg. In another shallow plate combine crumbs and Parmesan cheese, blending well. Cut meat into 4 pieces; pound to ¼ inch. Dip in egg and coat. Arrange in 1½ quart baking dish. Top meat with onion and cover with waxed paper.

Cook at 100% power for 4 - 8 minutes until meat is partially cooked. Top with cheese slices, then spoon tomato sauce over top and sprinkle with pepper and Italian spices. Cook, covered with waxed paper for 4 - 6 minutes at 50% power until bubbly. Sprinkle with Parmesan cheese and cook another 30 seconds to melt cheese. 4 servings. (This casserole may be made ahead and refrigerated. You will need to increase cooking time a minute or two if cold.) *Beef round steak, cut ¼ inch thick can be used for veal.

FISH AND SEAFOOD

BAKED FISH FILLETS

1½ - 2 lbs. fish fillets
Cayenne pepper
1 Tbsp. lemon juice
⅛ tsp. paprika
2 Tbsp. butter
2 Tbsp. flour

1 c. milk
1 tsp. salt
Dash garlic powder
¼ c. bread crumbs
1 Tbsp. chopped parsley

Season fish with pepper and place in a flat baking dish. Top with the lemon juice and paprika. In a 4 cup measure melt butter for 1 minute at 100% power. Add flour, salt and garlic powder. Slowly stir in the milk. Cook at 100% power* for 2 - 3 minutes until thick. Pour over fish and sprinkle with bread crumbs and parsley. Microwave, uncovered, at 50% power for 15 minutes, rotating if necessary. *Preferable to cook this at 70% power for 4 - 5 minutes if time allows.

GOLDEN FISH FILLETS

1 - 1½ lb. fish fillets
½ - ¾ c. Italian bread crumbs
Paprika

Black pepper
¼ c. butter, melted

Place the crumbs in a shallow plate and bread the fish on both sides. Arrange the fillets in a circle on a serving dish or baking rack. Do not put a fillet in the center of the plate. Remember that the circle lets the microwaves enter the fish from all sides (outside and inside and up and down). This way they will never have to be turned or rearranged as they will cook evenly. Drizzle the butter over the fillets and cook covered with a paper towel for 3 minutes per pound. The paper towel is used to prevent splatter. Since the dish is to be "crusty" you would not use a cover if conventionally cooking the fish. That is why our "no lid" which we consider the paper towel is used ... as we use the same technique in microwave cooking as in conventional cooking.

RED SNAPPER FILLETS WITH ARTICHOKES

6 (2 - 2½ lbs.) red snapper fillets
½ c. butter
4 Tbsp. chopped green onion
    tops
2 Tbsp. chopped parsley
3 cloves garlic, minced
1 Tbsp. lemon juice

4 oz. fresh mushrooms, sliced
1 (14 oz.) can artichoke hearts,
    drained and sliced
1 tsp. salt
½ tsp. cayenne pepper
¼ tsp. basil

86

Dry fillets with paper towels and place in flat baking dish in a 4 cup measure, saute onions, garlic, parsley for 1½ - 2 minutes at 100% power. Add lemon, mushrooms, artichokes and spices. Microwave for 2 minutes at 100% power until heated through. Top fillets with sauce and cover with waxed paper. Cook for 7 - 8 minutes at 100% power until fish flakes easily. Let stand covered for 3 - 4 minutes. (Allow 3 - 5 minutes per pound for fish.)

CRAB BAKED AVOCADOS

3 Tbsp. margarine
2 c. chopped onion
½ c. cream
1 tsp. salt
¼ tsp. cayenne pepper
⅛ tsp. paprika
1 lb. lump crab meat

½ c. seasoned bread crumbs
5 or 6 ripe avocados, room temp.
Lemon slice
1 c. (4 oz.) finely chopped Cheddar cheese
Parsley

Cook onion for 5 minutes at 100% power covered. Into the onions stir the cream, spices, crab and crumbs. Cover and cook for 2 minutes at 100% power. Set aside until ready to stuff avocados. Halve avocados. Peel, if desired, but skin may be left on to help retain shape better. Spoon crab mixture into avocados and sprinkle with cheese. Arrange 5 or 6 stuffed avocado halves in a circle in shallow baking dish. Microwave first dish for 2 minutes at 100% power while you are arranging next dish in similar fashion. Microwave second dish for same time. Serve hot garnished with parsley. Avocados may also be microwaved for 30 seconds at 100% power in individual plates, if desired.

CRAB ENCHILADAS

2 Tbsp. margarine
1 c. chopped onion
1 (10 oz.) can tomatoes and green chilies, chopped
1 (8 oz.) can tomato sauce
1 tsp. chili powder

½ tsp. oregano
¼ tsp. cumin, optional
½ tsp. salt
Dash cayenne pepper
12 soft corn tortillas
Sour cream

Filling:

1 lb. white crabmeat
⅓ c. ripe olives

2 c. (8 oz.) grated Monterey Jack cheese, divided

Melt margarine for 30 seconds at 100% power in 4 cup container. Stir in onion and saute at 100% power for 3 minutes. Add tomatoes and green chilies, tomato sauce, chili powder and spices. Mix well and bring to boil at 100% power, about 2 - 2½ minutes. Cover with paper towel and microwave for 4 minutes at 100% power until flavors blend. Let stand covered. Combine crabmeat, 1 cup cheese, olives and ½ c. sauce. Mix well. Dip each tortilla in warm sauce. In a 7 x 11 inch baking dish place tortillas, seam side down, which have been filled with equal portions of meat filling. Spoon remaining sauce over top and sprinkle with remaining cheese. Microwave for 5 minutes at 100% power.* Rotate dish if necessary for even cooking. Serve topped with sour cream.

      * If time permits lower temperature to 70% power and cook for about 8 minutes. Foods with dairy products and cheese are much more successful with a lower heat.

LOBSTER TAILS

2 (8 to 10 oz.) lobster tails, thawed	1 Tbsp. butter
	1 tsp. lemon juice

      Place the lobster tails in a baking dish underside up. Cover tightly with plastic wrap and microwave for 2½ minutes at 100% power. Remove from the dish and cut through the backs of the shells and partially through the meat, but leaving shell intact. Spread shell and loosen meat with fingers. Brush the lobster meat with the butter/lemon mixture. Covered and top sides up, cook an additional 3 minutes. Meat should be lightly translucent. *Do not overcook!* The meat finishes cooking during the standing time. That is why you must cook to only 80% done on all food as the food cooks 20% while standing.

AVOCADO AND SCALLOPS DIVINE

2 lbs. scallops	¼ tsp. thyme
¾ c. dry white wine	1 bay leaf
¾ c. scallop liquid	½ lb. fresh mushrooms, sliced
¼ c. minced onion	3 ripe avocados, halved
½ tsp. salt	

      Sauce:

¼ c. butter	¼ tsp. salt
¼ c. flour	⅛ tsp. white pepper
1½ c. stock from scallops	
¼ c. whipping cream	
⅔ c. mayonnaise, scant, to which 2 - 3 Tbsp. lemon juice has been added	

      Cut scallops into large bite size pieces. Place in 1½ qt. dish, cover with plastic wrap and cook for 8 - 10 minutes at 100% power, stirring once to rearrange. Drain and measure ¾ c. liquid. Cover scallops to keep warm. In 2 qt. bowl combine wine, liquid, onion, parsley and remaining spices. Microwave for 3 minutes at 100% power. Stir in mushrooms and scallops. Cover and microwave for 3 minutes at 100% power. Test scallop for doneness after one minute. Should be flaky. Strain and reserve 1½ c. stock for sauce. Set scallops aside covered. In an 8 cup measure, melt margarine for 30 - 45 seconds at 100%

power. Add flour and gradually stir in stock. Microwave at 100% power for 5 - 6 minutes until thickened, stirring occasionally. Stir in cream, mayonnaise and lemon, salt and pepper. Combine all. Fill peeled avocado halves with mixture and serve immediately.

SHRIMP CASSEROLE

¾ lb. shrimp, peeled and
   deveined*
⅓ c. chopped celery
¼ c. chopped green pepper
¼ c. chopped onion
1 Tbsp. butter, optional
1 can (10¾ oz.) condensed
   cream of mushroom soup

⅓ c. sliced water chestnuts
1 hard cooked egg, chopped
1 Tbsp. lemon juice
¼ tsp. salt
½ c. dry stuffing mix
¼ c. shredded Cheddar cheese

Thaw shrimp, if frozen. Cut large shrimp in half. In 1½ qt. shallow casserole dish combine shrimp, celery, green pepper, onion and butter. Cover and cook at 100% power for 4 minutes, stirring half way through cooking time. Stir in remaining ingredients except cheese. Cover and cook at 100% power for an additional 4 minutes. Rotate if necessary. Sprinkle cheese on top of casserole and cook, uncovered, at 70% power for 1 - 1½ minutes. * If precooked shrimp is used, add during second cooking time.

SHRIMP GUMBO

⅔ c. flour
⅔ c. oil
2 c. chopped onion
1 c. chopped celery
½ c. chopped green pepper
1 - 2 c. sliced okra
4 cloves garlic, minced
¼ c. chopped parsley

2 lbs. shrimp, raw, peeled
2 tsp. gumbo file
1 can tomato paste
2 tsp. salt
1 tsp. cayenne pepper
½ tsp. pepper
1 - 1½ qts. hot water
¼ c. chopped green onion tops

Mix oil and flour together in a 4 cup measure to make a roux. Cook at 100% power for 6 - 7 minutes until dark brown. Add onion, celery, green pepper, okra, garlic and parsley to roux. Transfer this to 4 qt. casserole. Cook additional 4 - 5 minutes at 100% power. Add shrimp, tomato paste, spices, hot water. Cook at 100% power for 16 minutes, stirring every 5 minutes. Add file. Sprinkle onion tops on gumbo before serving over rice. Pass additional file, if desired.

STEAMED SHRIMP

**1 lb. shrimp, fresh or frozen and
defrosted
½ tsp. cayenne**

**½ lemon, sliced
½ tsp. basil
Dash garlic powder**

Place shrimp in circle fashion, uniform depth, on glass dish.* Sprinkle with herbs (your favorites may be used in place of suggested ones). Cover with waxed paper, cook for 3 - 4 min. per pound at 100% power, rearranging if cooking is not uniform. DO NOT OVERCOOK. Shrimp will be pink when done. Add salt during standing time, if desired.

* Ring mold works very well.

notes:

_____
_____
_____
_____
_____
_____
_____
_____
_____
_____
_____
_____
_____
_____
_____
_____
_____
_____
_____
_____
_____
_____
_____
_____

Desserts and Sweets

DID YOU KNOW?

Do not frost cakes until cool.

Baking powder biscuits will have better texture if you knead the dough for half a minute after mixing.

A dash of Worcestershire sauce adds zip to hot mulled cider, pumpkin pie, spiced cookies and cakes.

Measure liquid shortening into measuring cup first before sticky substance such as honey is added and it will pour out easily.

Cookies, graham crackers and sugar-type cereal that remain in the bottom of their containers as pieces may be placed in a food processor and reduced to crumbs. Save in either a tightly closed container or freeze for use later as "great" pie crusts or to extend chopped nuts on desserts for topping.

Crackers, bread, chips and regular cereals may also be reduced to crumbs in the food processor and kept for casserole toppings and crumb coatings.

Coat berries, raisins or nuts with flour before adding to batter to prevent them from sinking to the bottom.

A cake that is lightly buttered on top while cooling will not get crumbly when you frost the completely cooled cake.

Use powdered gelatin mix for colored sugar when decorating baked goods.

Use stuffing cubes as breadcrumbs for meatloaves and meatballs for less mess.

Cookie dough stored in cans in the refrigerator or freezer can be pushed out for easy slicing after removing second end from can.

Dip cheese slicer in flour to cut uniform cookies from a roll of dough.

Sift dry cake mix before you add other ingredients so it won't be lumpy.

Store peanut butter upside down so oils stay mixed with nuts.

So they will be easy to remove from the pan, place a pie or cake on a wet hot towel for a few minutes.

CANDY AND FROSTING CHARTS

	Temperature of Syrup
Thread	230-234 degrees
Soft ball	234-240 degrees
Firm ball	244-248 degrees
Hard ball	250-266 degrees
Hard crack	300-310 degrees

DESSERTS AND SWEETS
BARS AND COOKIES

FIRST PRIZE BROWNIES

4 sq. (4 oz.) bittersweet
    chocolate
1 c. (2 sticks) butter
1 c. white sugar
1 c. brown sugar
4 eggs, room temperature
1 c. all purpose flour

2 tsp. vanilla
1 tsp. baking soda, optional
1/8 tsp. salt
3/4 c. pecans
1 c. milk, optional
1 c. chocolate chips, optional

Melt chocolate and butter in 8 cup measure for 3 - 3½ minutes at 100% power. Stir in sugar, blending well. Beat in eggs one at a time. Stir in flour* and vanilla. Blend in chips and nuts. Place in 8 x 12'' greased baking dish or two smaller pans. Bake for 8 - 10 minutes at 50% power and 2 - 4 minutes at 100% power, turning if necessary for even cooking. * Baking soda and milk are added here, if cakier brownies are desired. May also cook at 70% power for 6 - 7 minutes.

FRUIT CHEWY BROWNIES

2 eggs
1 c. sugar
2/3 c. butter, melted
1 tsp. vanilla
3/4 c. flour
1/3 c. unsweetened cocoa

1 tsp. baking powder
1/2 tsp. salt
1½ c. fresh Bartlett pears,
    coarsely chopped
1/2 c. walnuts or pecans,
    chopped

Beat eggs and blend in sugar, butter and vanilla. Beat until sugar is dissolved. Combine flour, cocoa, baking powder and salt and stir into egg mixture until flour is evenly moistened and batter is smooth. Fold in pears and nuts and pour into 9 inch baking dish. Microwave at 70% power for 6 minutes. Cook an additional 3 - 4 minutes, turning when necessary. Cool and cut.

BROWNIE PIE

1/3 c. butter
2 squares unsweetened
    chocolate
1 c. sugar
2 eggs, slightly beaten

3/4 c. flour
1/4 tsp. baking powder
1/4 tsp. salt
1 tsp. vanilla
1/2 c. chopped nuts

Place chocolate and butter in 4 cup measure. Cook 50% power for 1½ - 2 min. Stir in sugar. Add a small amount of hot mixture into eggs and return to hot mixture. * Stir in flour, baking powder, salt, vanilla and nuts. Spread in a 2 qt. round dish, lightly greased. Cook 50% power for 5 - 7 minutes. Turn two times, if necessary. Finish at 100% power for 1 - 3 minutes. ** Cool and cut into wedges. Serve with ice cream and hot fudge sauce, if desired.

* This prevents eggs from curdling. ** May also cook 70% for about 6 - 7 minutes.

CHOCOLATE CHIP COOKIES

½ c. butter or margarine
⅔ c. brown sugar
1 egg
1 tsp. soda
1 tsp. vanilla

¼ tsp. salt
1¾ c. flour
½ c. chocolate chips
¼ c. nuts, optional

Mix butter, sugar, egg, soda, vanilla and salt until light and fluffy. Stir in remaining ingredients. Drop teaspoon full on wax paper in circle on baking sheet or plate. (7 cookies at a time.) * Microwave for 1½ - 2 minutes at 50% power. Cookies will not look done, but will finish cooking and harden as they cool. DO NOT OVERCOOK. Cool completely before removing from wax paper. * To proceed with baking, simply pull wax paper off baking sheet, replace with new waxed paper and proceed as above.

CHOCOLATE CHIP SQUARES

½ c. (1 stick) margarine
1 tsp. vanilla
⅔ c. packed brown sugar
1 egg
1¼ c. flour

1 tsp. baking powder
¼ tsp. salt
1 pkg. (6 oz.) semi-sweet
    chocolate pieces

Cream butter and vanilla. Add brown sugar and beat until fluffy. Add egg and beat thoroughly. Blend in flour, baking powder, salt. Stir well and stir in half of chocolate pieces. Turn into an ungreased 1½ quart baking dish. Top with remaining chocolate pieces. Cook uncovered at 70% power for 7 - 8 minutes until edges start to pull away from the sides. Rotate if necessary for even cooking. Set dish on a flat surface to cool, then cut into squares.

CHOCOLATE CHIP MARBLE BARS

½ c. butter
1 c. plus 2 Tbsp. flour, sifted
½ tsp. baking soda
½ tsp. salt
6 Tbsp. granulated sugar
6 Tbsp. brown sugar

½ tsp. vanilla
¼ tsp. water
1 egg
½ c. nuts, optional
1 pkg. (6 oz.) chocolate chips

In 8 cup measure soften butter for 1 minute at 50% power. Sift together dry ingredients and set aside. Blend butter with sugar, vanilla, water and egg. Add flour mixture and mix well. Stir in nuts. Spread evenly in 8 x 12" or equivalent size round pan. Sprinkle with chocolate chips. Microwave for 4 - 5 minutes at 50% power until chips are soft enough to marbleize by running a knife through the surface of the dough. Microwave at 70% for 7 - 8 minutes, turning if necessary until done, but center still slightly moist. Bars will firm while cooling.

CHOCOLATE/SCOTCH BARS

½ c. margarine
⅔ c. packed brown sugar
2 c. quick cooking rolled oats

½ c. chopped nuts*
1 tsp. vanilla

Topping:

½ c. chocolate chips

¼ c. peanut butter

In 1½ or 2 qt. container microwave margarine for 45 - 60 seconds at 100% power until melted. Blend in sugar and stir in remaining ingredients. Spread into greased 8 x 8 inch baking dish or round dish of same capacity. Place dish elevated slightly in microwave and cook for 4 - 8 minutes at 70% power until bubbly all over. Rotate if necessary for even cooking. Cool 2 minutes and sprinkle with chips. Drop small drops of peanut butter around on chips. When chocolate and peanut butter begin to melt spread, marbleizing slightly, to frost. Allow frosting to partially set and then cut into pieces. * ½ c. coconut may be used instead of nuts.

CRAZY COOKIES

¼ c. margarine
¾ c. graham cracker crumbs
½ c. peanut butter morsels
½ c. chocolate morsels

1 c. shredded coconut
½ c. chopped nuts
1 can (14 oz.) sweetened
    condensed milk

Place butter in 8 x 8 x 2" baking dish. Microwave for 45 seconds to 1 minute at 100% power until melted. Stir in graham cracker crumbs and mix until blended. Press evenly in bottom of dish and microwave for 2 - 3 minutes at 100% power until set. Turn half way through if needed for even cooking. Next, layer each of the remaining ingredients in listed order. Microwave at 50% power for 6 - 8 minutes until bubbly. Allow to stand on a solid surface until cooled completely. Cut into bars.

CREME DE MENTHE BARS

Base:

2 squares (1 oz.) unsweetened
   chocolate
½ c. butter
½ c. sugar
½ c. brown sugar

2 eggs
1 tsp. vanilla
⅔ c. unsifted flour
½ tsp. baking powder

Filling:

½ c. butter
2 c. powdered sugar
2 Tbsp. green creme de menthe

4 drops green food color
¼ tsp. peppermint extract

Frosting:

1 c. (6 oz.) semi-sweet chocolate
   chips

2 Tbsp. cooking oil

In glass mixing bowl microwave chocolate and butter for 1 - 1½ minutes at 100% power until melted. Stir until smooth. Blend in sugar and beat in eggs, one at a time. Stir in remaining base ingredients and spread in 12 x 8 inch baking dish. Cover with waxed paper and microwave for 4 - 6 minutes at 100% power until surface is no longer doughy. Cool completely.

In small dish microwave butter at 100% power for 15 - 30 seconds until soft. Add powdered sugar. Mix well and gradually add remaining filling ingredients. Beat until creamy and spread evenly over cooled base. Refrigerate to set filling.

Combine frosting ingredients in 2 cup measure and microwave at 100% power, uncovered, for 1½ - 2 minutes. Stir until smooth and spread evenly over filling. Refrigerate to set. Store in refrigerator but allow to stand at room temperature for 10 minutes before cutting.

LEMON CHEESECAKE BARS

½ c. margarine
½ c. packed brown sugar
¼ tsp. salt
1 c. quick cooking rolled oats
1 c. all-purpose flour
1 pkg. (8 oz.) cream cheese

⅓ c. granulated sugar
1 egg
1 Tbsp. grated lemon peel
1 Tbsp. lemon juice
2 Tbsp. milk
½ tsp. cinnamon, optional

Mix margarine, sugar and salt. Add the oats and flour and beat at low speed until ingredients are quite fine. Reserve one cup and press the remaining mixture in an 8 x 8 inch baking dish. Microwave at 50% power for 3 - 8 minutes. Cook until done, but do not overcook. Turn dish if necessary for even cooking. Microwave cream cheese for 30 seconds at 50% power. Mix cheese and remaining ingredients, blending well. Spread over base and sprinkle with remaining crumb mixture. Microwave at 100% power for 6 - 10 minutes until center is set, turning for even cooking if necessary. Cool and refrigerate before serving.

MARSHMALLOW-BUTTERSCOTCH BARS

¼ c. butter
½ c. peanut butter
1 pkg. (10 oz.) marshmallows,
    small or cut in pieces
4 - 5 c. rice crisp cereal

1 pkg. (6 oz.) semi-sweet
    chocolate pieces
1 pkg. (6 oz.) peanut butter
    pieces

Put butter, peanut butter and marshmallows in a 2 qt. measure. Cook uncovered for 1½ - 2 minutes at 70% power or until melted. Stir until smooth. Mix cereal into marshmallow mixture and press into lightly buttered 1½ qt. baking dish. Combine chocolate and peanut butter pieces in 1 qt. measure and melt in microwave for 4 - 5 minutes at 50% power. Stir until smooth and spread over cereal. Cool until set. Makes about 12 bars.

NUT SQUARES

Crust:

½ c. butter
½ c. packed brown sugar
¾ c. quick cooking rolled oats

½ c. flour
¼ tsp. soda

Topping:

1 c. butterscotch pieces
¼ c. light corn syrup

1 Tbsp. butter
1¼ c. (6 oz.) mixed nuts

Microwave butter at 100% power for 15 - 30 seconds in 8 cup measure. Add sugar and blend until creamy. Add oats, flour and soda and mix well. Using a fork, press mixture evenly into an ungreased 8 inch microwave safe dish. Microwave at 100% power, uncovered, for 3 - 4 minutes or until puffed throughout, but no longer doughy, rotating if necessary. Combine butterscotch pieces, corn syrup and butter in 2 cup measure. Microwave at 100% power uncovered, for 1 - 1½ minutes until chips are melted, stirring once. Sprinkle nuts over base. Pour butterscotch pieces evenly over nuts. * Cool completely and cut into small pieces. * Peanuts may be substituted for mixed nuts and chocolate pieces for butterscotch if desired.

CRUNCHY PEANUT BARS

1 c. light corn syrup
1 c. brown sugar, packed well
1 c. peanut butter
6 c. corn flake cereal

1 c. salted peanuts
1 c. (6 oz.) milk chocolate pieces
1 Tbsp. cooking oil

Combine the syrup and brown sugar in a 2 qt. measure. Microwave for 3 - 4 minutes at 100% power until the mixture boils. Stir in peanut butter until blended, then cereal and nuts. Mix only to coat. Press into a greased 12 x 8 or 13 x 9" pan. Combine the oil and chocolate pieces into a 2 cup measure and microwave uncovered for 2 - 4 minutes at 50% power until softened. Stir until smooth and spoon onto bars. Spread evenly and refrigerate for one hour or until set. Store in cool place.

TOFFEE GRAHAMS

1 Tbsp. butter
9 graham cracker squares
½ c. butter
½ c. packed brown sugar

½ c. chopped nuts
½ c. semi-sweet or milk
    chocolate chips

Melt 1 Tbsp. butter in 8 x 8 inch baking dish for about 30 - 45 seconds at 100% power. Spread evenly and line bottom of the dish with cracker squares, cutting when necessary to fit. Combine the butter and sugar in a 4 cup measure and microwave at 100% power for 1 minute. Beat until smooth. Microwave for 1 - 2 more minutes until very hot. Pour over the crackers and spread. Sprinkle with nuts and cook for another 1½ - 3 minutes at 100% until the mixture boils for a minute. Cool for 2 minutes and sprinkle with chocolate. When soft, spread to frost. Loosen edges and cut into quarters to remove. Cut into smaller serving pieces. Can store in refrigerator if you wish these crisp.

CAKES AND FROSTINGS

AMARETTO BUNDT CAKE

1 (18½ oz.) box yellow cake mix
1 (3¾ oz.) box instant vanilla
   pudding
2 (7 oz.) pkg. almond paste
   crumbled

⅓ c. chopped pecans
4 eggs
½ c. vegetable oil
½ c. Amaretto liqueur
¼ c. water

Glaze:

½ c. butter
½ c. sugar
¼ c. Amaretto liqueur

¼ c. water
2 - 3 drops of red food color,
   optional

Grease bundt pan and sprinkle with pecans. Set aside. Mix cake and pudding mix with crumbled almond paste in a processor. After this is well blended place in 8 cup measure and mix with eggs, oil, liqueur and water. Beat very well with electric mixer. Pour batter into cake pan and microwave at 70% power for 13 - 15 minutes, turning if necessary for even cooking. Cool cake for 10 minutes before topping with glaze. While the cake is cooling, melt butter in 4 cup measure for 1 minute at 100% power. Add the sugar, liqueur and water and bring this to a boil, about 2 minutes at 100% power. Make slits or small holes in cake before you take it out of pan. Let this stand several hours before turning out.

APPLE FLAMBE

1 pkg. (17½ oz.) apple cake mix*

1 can apple pie filling (more if
   desired)*
8 oz. frozen whipped topping,
   thawed

2 fresh apples, sliced
Cinnamon
Lemon rind shavings
1 Tbsp. butter, optional
2 oz. brandy

Mix cake according to directions and bake each 8 inch cake layer for 7 - 8 minutes at 70% power. Cool. Split each layer into two thin layers. Place first layer on cake plate and spread with apple pie filling, sprinkle with cinnamon and lemon shavings. Repeat with each layer of cake. Cook sliced apples in 4 cup measure with a bit of cinnamon for 2 - 3 minutes covered. Pipe outer edge of top layer of cake with whipped topping. Arrange apples in decorative design or swirl in center of top layer. Heat brandy in microwave in 1 or 2 cup container for 30 - 45 seconds at 100% power. Light brandy and pour flaming over apples. Serve immediately.

* May use different flavors of cake and fillings, if desired.

APRICOT CRUMBLE

2 c. flour
1 c. sugar
½ c. butter, softened
2 tsp. cinnamon

2 tsp. baking powder
2 eggs
¾ c. unsweetened apricot juice

Mix flour, sugar and butter together with fork until crumbly. For crumb topping remove 1 cup of mixture and stir in cinnamon and reserve. Stir baking powder into large crumbed mixture. Whisk eggs with juice and mix lightly into crumb mixture. Lightly grease a 2 quart casserole or bundt dish. Pour in mixture and sprinkle on crumb topping. Microwave at 50% power for 8 minutes, turning once. Finish cooking on 100% power for 1 - 2 minutes or 9 - 11 minutes at 70% power.

BUTTER CROWN POUND CAKE

Topping:

⅓ c. margarine
2 Tbsp. brown sugar
½ c. pecans, chopped

¾ c. crushed vanilla wafers
   (approximately 15)

Cake:

½ c. margarine
1 c. sugar
2 eggs
½ c. milk

½ tsp. vanilla
1¼ c. flour
½ tsp. baking powder
⅛ tsp. salt

Soften butter for 20 seconds at 100% power. Stir in brown sugar, pecans and wafers until blended. Grease bottom and sides of 8 x 4" or 9 x 5 inch loaf dish*, lined with waxed paper. Pat topping evenly into bottom and up sides of pan. Set aside.

Microwave butter for 20 - 25 seconds at 100% power until soft. Mix butter and sugar. Add eggs, beating well. Add remaining ingredients and mix until smooth. Pour into pan, spreading evenly. Bake uncovered for 10 minutes at 50% power. Rotate and cook an additional 2 - 3 minutes at 100% power. Cool for 10 - 15 minutes. Loosen edges gently with knife. Invert onto plate and peel off waxed paper. * Mini bundt pan may also be used for baking. This cake is excellent with Fudge Sauce listed in this book. 70% power can be used in this recipe also. (9 - 11 minutes)

CARROT CAKE

4 eggs
1¼ c. cooking oil
1 c. sugar
1 c. firmly packed brown sugar
1 can (8 oz.) crushed pineapple
    drained (reserve 2 Tbsp.
    juice)
2 c. flour

2 tsp. cinnamon
½ tsp. allspice
1½ tsp. baking powder
1½ tsp. soda
1 tsp. salt
3 c. shredded carrots
½ c. nuts

    Icing:

1 pkg. (8 oz.) cream cheese
½ c. powdered sugar

1 - 2 Tbsp. pineapple juice

Beat eggs until frothy. Add oil and sugars and beat until smooth. Blend in remaining ingredients except topping and mix well. Lightly oil a 12 cup fluted cake pan and sprinkle with sugar-cinnamon, removing any excess. Spoon batter into pan. Microwave 70% power for 12 - 14 minutes until surface is no longer doughy. Cool 10 minutes and invert onto serving plate.

AMARETTO SWIRL CHEESECAKE

    Crust:

¼ c. margarine
1 c. (approx. 12 squares)
    graham cracker crumbs

2 Tbsp. sugar
¼ tsp. cinnamon

    Filling:

2 pkgs. (8 oz.) cream cheese
⅔ c. sugar
3 eggs
1 c. sour cream
1 tsp. vanilla

2 Tbsp. unsweetened cocoa
2 Tbsp. sugar
3 Tbsp. Amaretto or favorite
    liqueur

In 9" quiche or in deep 9 inch pie plate microwave butter for 30 - 45 seconds at 100% power until melted. Stir in crumbs, sugar and cinnamon and press into dish to form pie crust. * Set aside.

Soften cream cheese in 1 qt. for 30 seconds to 1 minute at 70% - 100% power. Beat until creamy and add ⅔ c. sugar. Mix in eggs one at a time, mixing well. Blend in sour cream and vanilla. Pour half (about 2 cups) of mixture into crust. Combine cocoa and 2 Tbsp. sugar, mix well. Add to remaining mixture along with Amaretto (or flavor of your choice). Mix well and pour over vanilla filling. Swirl chocolate through vanilla. Microwave at 50% power for 15 - 18 minutes or until center is almost set. Cool and refrigerate at least 6 hours before serving. Store covered in refrigerator. * You may place crumbs in bottom of pan only if you wish cheesecake to resemble that of one baked in spring mold.

PRALINE CHEESECAKE

1 c. graham cracker crumbs
   (about 14 double crackers)
¼ c. (½ stick) butter, melted
1½ lbs. cream cheese
1½ tsp. vanilla

1¼ c. brown sugar, firmly
   packed
3 eggs
1 c. chopped pecans
2 Tbsp. flour

Topping:

½ c. brown sugar, firmly packed
¼ c. (½ stick) butter

12 pecan halves

Combine crumbs and butter in 9 inch quiche or tart pan. Microwave for 30 - 45 seconds at 100% power until butter is melted. Press evenly in bottom of pan. Blend cream cheese and brown sugar in 8 cup measure until well blended. Add eggs one at a time, beating well after each addition. Stir in pecans, flour and vanilla, mixing thoroughly. Turn into pan, spreading evenly. Cook 18 - 20 minutes at 50% power, rotating if necessary for even cooking. Let cheesecake cool to room temperature and refrigerate overnight. For topping combine sugar and butter in 2 cup measure and cook at 100% power for about 1 - 1½ min. until smooth and thickened. Pour the hot topping over the chilled cake, spreading to cover top. Decorate edge with pecan halves. Serve chilled or at room temperature. Note that miscellaneous desserts are cooked by a comparable method in the microwave as in conventional cooking (temperature, covers, etc.).

CHERRY NUT CAKE

1 (9 oz.) cake mix or 2 cups
   favorite batter
1 can cherry pie filling*

2 Tbsp. margarine
½ c. nuts, chopped

Mix cake mix according to directions, except using a tablespoon or two less water and set aside. Cut a circle of wax paper and fit into bottom of cake pan. Grease sides and pat with crushed nuts. Pour in pie filling and top with batter. Microwave for 9 - 12 minutes at 70% power. * You may use any flavor of cake mix or pie filling you wish. Notice that we use a bit less liquid when converting conventional recipes to microwave. This is due to the fact there is very little evaporation and less water is needed.

SELF-ICING CHOCOLATE CAKE

1 (17 - 18 oz.) pkg. chocolate
  cake mix
1 (3 oz.) pkg. instant chocolate
  pudding
1½ c. milk

2 eggs
½ c. chopped pecans, optional
1 (12 oz.) pkg. semi-sweet
  chocolate chips

Blend cake mix, pudding, milk, eggs, pecans and chocolate. Pour into a greased 10 inch tube pan. Microwave at 100% power for 9 - 14 minutes. * Turn if needed during cooking. Allow cake to cool for 5 - 10 minutes before inverting onto serving platter. Spread melted chocolate on top or you may let cool and sprinkle with powdered sugar. 8 - 10 servings. * If time allows, you may try cooking this cake at 70% power for 12 - 18 minutes. This temperature relates to conventional temperature. Therefore keep our techniques similar.

CRANBERRY CAKE WITH BUTTER RUM SAUCE

¼ c. margarine
1 c. sugar
1 c. milk
1 tsp. vanilla
2 c. flour
2 tsp. baking powder

⅛ tsp. salt
½ tsp. each cinnamon and
  nutmeg
2 c. fresh cranberries
1 tsp. sugar
¼ tsp. cinnamon

Sauce:

½ c. butter
1 c. sugar
½ c. evaporated milk

½ tsp. vanilla
1 Tbsp. rum flavoring

In 8 cup measure melt butter for 30 - 45 seconds at 100% power. Blend in sugar, milk and vanilla (may look curdled). Add baking powder, flour, salt and spices. Beat until smooth and fold in cranberries. Grease bottom of ring mold baking dish and sprinkle with sugar and cinnamon. Pour in batter and microwave at 50% power for 18 - 20 minutes. * Rotate if necessary and microwave additional 1 - 3 minutes at 100% power. Serve warm or cool.

* Or 11 - 12 minutes at 70% power.

Sauce: Melt butter uncovered in 1 qt. measure for 7 - 9 minutes at 70 - 100% power. Stir occasionally until lightly browned. Stir in sugar. Gradually blend in milk and microwave for 1½ - 2 minutes at 50 - 70% power until boiling, stirring once. Stir in flavorings and serve over cake.

GINGERBREAD WITH LEMON BUTTER SAUCE

1¼ c. flour
⅓ c. brown sugar
½ tsp. soda
½ tsp. salt
½ tsp. cinnamon
½ tsp. ginger

¼ tsp. cloves
⅓ c. shortening
2 eggs
⅓ c. light molasses
¼ c. hot water
¼ tsp. mustard powder, opt.

Lemon Butter Sauce:

½ c. margarine
1 c. sugar
1 Tbsp. cornstarch
1 Tbsp. grated lemon rind

⅓ c. lemon juice
⅓ c. water
2 eggs, slightly beaten

Place all ingredients in mixing bowl and mix well. Spread in 8 or 9 inch round cake pan and bake at 50% power for 5 - 6 minutes. Increase up to 100% power and cook for 1 - 4 minutes. * Cool directly on counter top for 5 to 10 minutes. ** While cake is cooling, make lemon sauce by creaming butter, sugar and cornstarch. Blend in remaining ingredients. Microwave at 100% power for 3-6 minutes or until clear and thickened, stirring after 2 minutes and at end of cooking time. (Sauce may be made ahead and reheated if preferred). Serve over warm gingerbread.

** If you wish to decorate the top of this gingerbread you may place ½ c. dried coconut in a blender and blend until powdery, fold a 9 x 9 inch pieces of waxed paper several times, cut to 8 or 9 inch circle and cut small nicely shaped holes in it to make a doily when open. Place on top of warm gingerbread and sprinkle with coconut or powdered sugar. Remove paper carefully. * 6 - 8 minutes at 70% power for cooking this cake may be used to keep our techniques similar to conventional methods. (Remember -- 70% power relates to 325 - 350 degrees in conventional oven.)

ICE CREAM CONE CUPCAKES

1 box cake mix
Ice cream cones, flat bottoms

Prepared icing
Misc. candies and sprinkles

Mix cake mix according to directions, reducing liquid just slightly. Fill cones ⅔ - ¾ full ... according to effect you wish. Bake for 30 - 45 seconds at 100% power per cupcake. * Let stand and cool completely before frosting and decorating. Use your imagination when decorating to make cones look like ice cream cones. Get your children involved - let them decorate. * Cook only one to three cupcakes at a time. If they tend to fall over during cooking, set in egg poacher or cups to help balance. 100% power is used so cakes will rise very quickly.

Whipped cream freezes beautifully when a small amount of gelatin is added.

OATMEAL CAKE

1½ c. water
1 c. quick cooking oatmeal
1½ c. flour
1 tsp. soda
½ tsp. salt
1 tsp. cinnamon

1½ tsp. ground nutmeg
½ c. shortening
1 c. firmly packed brown sugar
1 c. sugar
2 eggs
1 tsp. vanilla

Heat water in a 4 cup measure until boiling, about 3 - 4 minutes at 100% power. Stir in oats and set aside to cool slightly. Cream shortening and sugars in mixing bowl. Add eggs, oats and vanilla. Stir in the dry ingredients and mix well. Sprinkle a 10'' bundt pan with a combination of sugar and cinnamon. Add batter and cook for 10 - 12 minutes at 70% power. Allow cake to stand 10 minutes before turning out onto serving plate.

DEEP DISH PINEAPPLE CRUMBLE

2 c. flour
1 c. sugar
½ c. butter, softened
2 tsp. cinnamon

2 tsp. baking powder
2 eggs
¾ c. unsweetened pineapple
    juice

Mix flour, sugar and butter together with a fork until crumbly. For crumb topping remove 1 cup of crumbly mixture, stir in cinnamon and reserve. Stir baking powder into large crumbled mixture. Whisk eggs with pineapple juice and mix lightly into crumb mixture. Lightly grease a 2 quart round casserole or bundt dish and pour in mixture. Sprinkle on crumb topping and microwave for 8 minutes at 50% power; turn if necessary and continue cooking for 1 - 2 minutes at 100% power, or 8 - 11 minutes at 70% power.

SNICKER CAKE

28 vanilla caramels
1 (15 oz.) can sweetened
    condensed milk
2 Tbsp. butter
1 (18 oz.) pkg. chocolate cake
    mix

1 c. water
3 eggs
1 c. pecans, finely chopped

Combine caramels, milk and 1 Tbsp. butter in 2½ quart container. Microwave for 4 minutes at 100% power, stirring once. Combine cake mix, water, eggs and remaining 1 Tbsp. butter. Beat well according to directions. Line two 8 x 8 inch baking dishes with parchment paper.* Do not trim paper. Spread ½ the batter on paper in pans. Top with caramel mixture and sprinkle with pecans. Spread remaining batter over pecan layer. Microwave 100% power each, 6 - 8 minutes. Rotate, if necessary every 4 minutes. Cool for 10 - 12 minutes and then invert cake onto serving platter. Pull off paper and cut into serving pieces. 12 - 16 servings. No paper is necessary if you plan to leave cake in pan to serve. * If more even cooking is desired, use round 9" pans. Remember square pans get four way cooking in corners and 3 way on sides (see chart).

STRAWBERRY CAKE

½ pkg. (10 oz.) frozen sliced
   strawberries
¼ c. butter
1 pkg. (9 oz.) layer size yellow
   cake mix

2 eggs
¼ c. water or juice
3 Tbsp. butter
1 c. unsifted powdered sugar

Defrost half of package of strawberries by covering one end with foil. Microwave 100% power for 1 - 1½ minutes. Freeze remainder. In 8 cup measure place ¼ c. butter and microwave ½ - 1 minute at 100% power. Add cake mix, eggs, liquid and ¼ c. strawberries. Beat until smooth. Grease bottom of 8 inch round baking dish. Pour batter into dish. Microwave uncovered 7 - 9 minutes, 70% power, turning if necessary for even cooking. Let stand 5 minutes. In 2 cup measure microwave 3 Tbsp. butter for ½ minute or until melted. Blend in powdered sugar and remaining ¼ cup strawberries. Beat until smooth. Spread on cake while still warm and garnish with fresh strawberries if desired.

SOUR CREAM CHOCOLATE ICING

6 oz. chocolate chips   ½ c. sour cream

Melt chocolate chips at 50% power for 2 - 3 minutes, uncovered, until soft. Mix with sour cream and spread on cake or brownies.

CANDIES

CHOCOLATE CRUNCH

1 pkg. (6 oz.) butterscotch chips
1 pkg. (6 oz.) chocolate chips
1 c. salted peanuts

1 c. ripple-style potato chips,
crushed

Place chocolate and butterscotch chips in 3 qt. bowl. Microwave at 50% power for 4 - 5 minutes, stirring occasionally. Stir in peanuts and potato chips. Drop by teaspoonfuls onto parchment paper. Cool until set. Freezes well.

CHOCOLATE-PEANUT BUTTER CLUSTERS

1 pkg. (6 oz.) chocolate morsels
1 pkg. (12 oz.) peanut butter
  morsels

1 pkg. (12 oz.) salted peanuts
½ c. peanut butter

In a 2 quart bowl combine morsels and microwave 50% power for 4 - 6 minutes. Stir and add peanut butter half way through. Stir in peanuts and drop by spoonfuls on wax paper or into small paper cups.

CHOCOLATE COVERED POTATO CHIPS

1 (7 oz.) can ripple potato chips
2 Tbsp. cooking oil

2 pkgs. (12 oz.) each milk
chocolate pieces

Place chocolate in 1 qt. glass bowl along with cooking oil. Microwave at 50% power, uncovered, for 4 - 7 minutes until chocolate melts and will stir into smooth sauce. Dip chips into chocolate, one at a time, leaving one end uncovered. Tap gently to remove excess chocolate. Place on wax paper. Repeat. Refrigerate chips until chocolate is set. Store in tightly covered container. If chocolate becomes too cool, microwave another ½ - 1 minute. (This makes great gifts!)

CHOCOLATE DIPPED STRAWBERRIES

6 oz. dark sweet chocolate
  coating
¼ tsp. favorite liqueur flavoring

1 pint fresh unhulled
strawberries, rinsed and
dried

Break or cut chocolate into several pieces and place in 2 cup measure. Cook at 50% power, uncovered, for 2½ - 3 minutes or until melted, stirring once or twice. Stir until smooth and add flavoring. Dip berries in chocolate (about ¾ of total fruit should be covered). Place top of strawberry stem end down on waxed paper. Place in refrigerator for 5 - 10 minutes until set. Refrigerate until served.

FUDGE

1 lb. confectioners sugar	½ c. butter
½ c. cocoa	1 Tbsp. vanilla
¼ c. milk	½ c. pecans, chopped

Blend sugar and cocoa in 3 quart bowl. Add milk and butter. DO NOT STIR. Microwave at 100% power for 2 minutes, then stir well. Add vanilla and nuts. Stir until blended. Pour into buttered 8 x 8 inch dish. Refrigerate until set. Cut into squares. Freezes well.

FUDGE FABULOUS

4½ c. sugar	16 large marshmallows
1 stick margarine	12 oz. "real" chocolate chips
Dash salt	1 lb. milk chocolate
1 large (13 oz.) can evaporated milk	2 tsp. vanilla
	Nuts, optional

Bring sugar, butter and milk to rolling boil and boil for about 1½ minute at 100% power. Remove from heat and add marshmallows and chocolate with flavoring. Stir until all melted and pour into buttered jelly roll pan. Makes 5 pounds.

GUMDROP CANDY

1 lb. almond bark	1 pkg. (16 oz.) spiced gumdrops
3 Tbsp. vegetable shortening	

Place bark and shortening in 3 quart bowl. Microwave 4 - 5 minutes, covered, at 50% power, until soft. Stir in gumdrops and spread in 8 x 8 inch dish lined on bottom with parchment paper. Cool in refrigerator and cut into squares. Freezes well.

HAYSTACKS

1 pkg. (6 oz.) butterscotch chips	1 can (4½ oz.) chow mein noodles
½ c. peanut butter	
½ c. peanuts	

Place chips and peanut butter in 2 quart container. Cover with waxed paper and microwave at 50% power for 3 - 5 minutes. Blend in peanuts and noodles. Drop by forkfuls onto waxed paper.

MARSHMALLOW CHOCOLATES

1 pkg. (12 oz.) chocolate chips
1 pkg. (6 oz.) butterscotch chips
2 Tbsp. butter or margarine
¼ c. peanut butter

1 pkg. (10½ oz.) miniature
   marshmallows
1 c. salted peanuts

Place chips, butter and peanut butter in 3 quart bowl. Microwave at 50% power for 4 - 5½ minutes, stirring after 3 minutes. Stir until smooth. Add marshmallows and peanuts. Spread into greased 8 x 8 inch dish. Cool in refrigerator and cut into squares. Freezes well.

MARSHMALLOW TREATS

1 pkg. (14 oz.) caramels
1 can sweetened condensed
   milk
Rice crisp cereal, crushed
Coconut
Nuts

Shredded chocolate
Toothpicks
Assorted fruit (banana, apple,
   strawberry, etc.)
Marshmallows (cut into pieces)

Place caramels and milk in bowl and cook at 50 - 70% power 5 - 8 minutes until mixture is soft and can be stirred together into smooth sauce. Dip pieces of marshmallow and fruit into sauce, roll in crushed rice crisp cereal, coconut, chocolate, nuts, etc., serve on toothpicks.

MILLIONAIRES

1 pkg. (14 oz.) caramels
2 Tbsp. milk

2 c. chopped pecans
1 pkg. (12 oz.) chocolate chips

Unwrap caramels and place in 3 qt. bowl. Add milk and microwave at 100% power for 2 - 4 minutes, stirring every minute. Stir until smooth and add pecans, mixing well. Drop by teaspoonfuls onto parchment paper. Cool and chill. In 3 quart bowl combine chips, microwave at 50% power until melted, about 5 - 7 minutes. Stir well. Dip caramel nut center into chocolate and return to parchment paper. Chill and store in refrigerator. Freezes well.

PEANUT BRITTLE

1 c. salted peanuts
1 c. granulated sugar
½ c. white corn syrup

1 tsp. butter
1 tsp. vanilla
1 tsp. baking soda

Combine the sugar and corn syrup in an 8 cup measure and cook for 4 minutes at 100% power. Add the peanuts and continue to cook another 3 - 4 minutes. Next, we add the butter and vanilla and continue to cook for an additional minute. Finally add the soda and gently stir until mixture is light and foamy. Pour and spread quickly on a greased, flexible baking sheet. Cool for a half hour or so and then break into small pieces to finish cooling. Store in an air tight container.

PEPPERMINT BARK

1 lb. almond bark   1 pkg. (7 oz.) peppermint candy

Break bark into pieces and place in 3 quart bowl. Microwave at 50% power for approximately 5 - 6 minutes until pieces are soft. Stir after 3 minutes. While bark is melting, process candy in food processor until it is a fine powder. Add candy to melted bark and stir well. Spread on parchment paper ⅛ to ¼ inch thick. Cool in refrigerator until hard. Break into pieces. Freezes well.

TINGLY CANDY

1 pkg. (6 oz.) butterscotch chips   4 c. crisp rice cereal
1 pkg. (6 oz.) chocolate chips

In quart bowl microwave chips at 50% power for 4 - 6 minutes, stirring after 3 minutes. Add cereal, stirring well. Drop by teaspoon to parchment. Cool until set. Freezes well.

TURTLES

1 lb. pecan halves
1 pkg. (14 oz.) caramels

1 pkg. (6 oz.) chocolate chips
1 Tbsp. cooking oil

Split pecan halves and arrange in groups of five, resembling turtle legs (4) and head (1). Place caramels on buttered pie plate (6 at a time in circle fashion) and microwave for 15 - 30 seconds at 100% power until softened, but not melted. Place soft caramels on "legs" and "head," pressing down to form body. Place chocolate morsels in 2 cup measure with oil and microwave for 2 - 3 minutes at 100% power until melted. Stir and spread about ½ tsp. of chocolate over each "turtle." Chill.

PIES

CRUMB CRUST

2 c. crumbs (cookie or graham)   2 tsp. sugar
6 Tbsp. (¾ stick) butter*

Mix sugar and crumbs in pie shell and place butter on top of crumbs. Microwave for 1 - 1½ minutes at 100% power until butter is melted. Mix well and press into pie plate to form a well shaped shell. Bake for 1½ minute at 100% power.

* Lower butter content if rich cookie crumbs, such as butter pecan, are used.

CHOCOLATE PIE

1 (6 oz.) pkg. semi-sweet   1 pie crust, baked (9'')
   chocolate chips   Whipped cream
2 Tbsp. sugar   Grated chocolate or chocolate
3 Tbsp. milk   curls
3 eggs, separated

Combine chocolate chips, sugar and milk in 1½ quart container and microwave at 50% power for 3 - 4 minutes, stirring once. Beat egg yolks. Stir small amount of chocolate mixture into yolks so yolks will not curdle. Next add yolk mixture into remaining chocolate. Beat whites until stiff. Fold whites into chocolate mixture and pour into baked and cooled shell. Chill until firm. Garnish with whipped cream and chocolate, grated or curls. This takes 9'' pie plate.

CHOCOLATE PECAN PIE

1 (9 inch) pie crust, baked   ¾ c. sugar
2 (1 oz.) squares unsweetened   3 eggs
   chocolate   1 tsp. vanilla
3 Tbsp. margarine   1 c. chopped pecans
1 c. corn syrup

Prepare your favorite pastry recipe or transfer a frozen pie crust into a 9 inch pie plate. Prick the crust and bake for 3 - 4 minutes at 90 to 100% power. Turn half way through cooking time.

In a 4 cup measure melt the chocolate and butter for 1½ minutes at 100% power, stirring once. Add sugar, syrup and mix well. Cook at 100% power for 2 more minutes. In a mixing bowl beat the eggs slightly and slowly, pour chocolate over eggs, stirring constantly. Add vanilla and nuts and pour into cooled pie shell. Microwave for 6 - 7 minutes at 50% power, turning every 2 to 3 minutes if cooking is uneven. Cool pie before serving and top with whipped cream if desired.

LIGHT AS A CLOUD CUSTARD PIE

1 can condensed sweet milk
1½ c. water
¼ tsp. salt
½ tsp. vanilla

3 eggs, well beaten
Nutmeg
Cookie crumb crust

Bring water to almost boiling (2 - 4 minutes at 100% power). Add milk and vanilla, stirring well. Add well beaten eggs and heat an additional 2 - 3 minutes at 50% until mixture is hot. Pour into cooked pie shell. Cook for 12 - 18 minutes at 50% power. Turn if pie cooks unevenly. Knife will come clean at edge when finished. Remove and cover with waxed paper. Will firm upon standing.

EASY SUNDAE ICE CREAM PIE

1 crumb pie crust
1 pint vanilla ice cream
1 pint chocolate ice cream
¼ c. flaked coconut
¼ c. corn syrup

¼ c. chunky peanut butter
2 Tbsp. chopped peanuts
Whipped cream and caramel
    sauce, optional

Place vanilla ice cream in microwave for about 1 minute to soften. Spread evenly into crust. Combine coconut, syrup and peanut butter. Mix well and swirl through ice cream. Next take chocolate ice cream and place in microwave for about 1 minute to soften and spread this over the swirled vanilla/peanut butter mixture. Top with caramel sauce if desired and sprinkle with nuts. Add puffs of whipped cream. Freeze until very firm. To serve let pie stand at room temperature for 15 minutes before cutting.

SOUR CREAM LEMON OR LIME PIE

1 c. sugar
¼ c. cornstarch
1¼ c. milk
3 egg yolks, slightly beaten
1 tsp. grated lemon rind

⅓ c. lemon or lime juice
¼ c. margarine
1 c. sour cream
1 graham cracker pie crust

In 2 quart container stir together sugar and cornstarch. Gradually stir in milk until smooth. Stir in eggs, rind and juice. Add margarine. Mix and cook at 70% power until boiling, about 2 - 4 minutes. Boil for 30 seconds to 1 minute.

Remove and cover mixture with plastic wrap. Refrigerate 40 - 50 minutes until cool, but not set. Fold in sour cream and turn into pie crust. Refrigerate at least 2 hours. Garnish with whipped cream.

IMPOSSIBLE PUMPKIN PIE

12 oz. evaporated milk	2 eggs
¾ c. sugar	1 can (16 oz.) pumpkin
½ c. buttermilk baking mix	2½ tsp. pumpkin pie spice
2 Tbsp. margarine	2 tsp. vanilla

Combine all ingredients and beat for 2 minutes with hand beater or process for 1 minute in blender. Grease a 9 inch pie plate and pour pumpkin mixture into pie plate. Microwave, uncovered for 6 - 8 minutes at 100% power until edge is set. Reduce power to 50% and cook for an additional 4 - 6 minutes until center is set, rotating if necessary. Cool and serve with whipped cream.

PUMPKIN PECAN PIE

1 (9 or 10'') crumb pie shell, baked and cooled	3 eggs, slightly beaten
¾ c. brown sugar	2 - 3 tsp. pumpkin pie spice
12 oz. pumpkin	¼ - ½ c. pecan bits
12 oz. half & half	1 Tbsp. flour
	Dash salt, optional

In 2 quart measure combine sugar, pumpkin, eggs and cream, spices and flour. Microwave for 6 - 9 minutes at 50% power until slightly thickened and very hot. Stir occasionally. Pour into cooled pie shell to about ¼ inch from top. Sprinkle with pecans. Cover with wax paper in oven and microwave 11 - 26 minutes (18) at 50% power until center is set. Cool completely. Place on warm, damp towel for a few minutes. Makes for easy removal of pie. Also while cooking, put wax paper on bottom of oven in case pie boils over.

CHEESECAKE TARTS

6 vanilla wafers	½ tsp. vanilla
1 (3 oz.) pkg. cream cheese	½ tsp. lemon juice
⅓ c. brown sugar	Sour cream, jam or pie filling
1 egg	Fresh fruit, optional

Soften cream cheese for 30 - 45 seconds at 100% power. Add sugar, egg, flavorings and beat until smooth. Place vanilla wafers in bottom of 6 baking cups and place in custard cups or circle baker. Microwave at 30% power for

7 minutes. Cool one hour and then refrigerate. Sprinkle with brown sugar and add a dollop of sour cream and piece of fresh fruit for garnish, or use fruit preserves or pie filling to top.

OTHER SWEETS

APPLE CRISP

1 c. flour
1 c. rolled oats
1 c. packed brown sugar
½ c. margarine
1¾ lb. (4 c.) tart apples, diced

1 c. sugar
¼ c. flour
½ tsp. cinnamon
¼ tsp. nutmeg

Mix flour, oats, sugar in large container. Stir in butter until crumbly mixture is formed and set aside. Combine apples, sugar, flour and spices in 8 x 8" baking dish. Stir to mix and sprinkle with topping. Microwave at 100% power for 10 - 12 minutes until apple mixture starts to bubble through topping. Delicious served with ice cream.

APPLE CHEESE CRISP

Filling 1:

6 c. apples, pared, sliced
1 Tbsp. lemon juice
⅓ c. sugar

3 Tbsp. flour, divided
½ tsp. cinnamon
¼ tsp. salt

Filling 2:

3 - 4 oz. cream cheese, softened
1 Tbsp. milk
¼ c. granulated sugar

1 egg
1 Tbsp. flour

Topping:

¼ c. plus 1 Tbsp. butter, melted
¼ c. brown sugar

¾ c. quick cooking rolled oats
¾ c. flour

Topping: Microwave butter at 100% power for 45 - 60 seconds. Stir in brown sugar and oats. Microwave for 2 minutes at 100% power. Stir in flour and set aside.

Filling 1: Combine apples, juice, ⅓ c. sugar, 2 Tbsp. flour, cinnamon and salt in 8" baking dish. Stir and spread in pan evenly. Microwave at 100% power for 8 minutes, stirring half way through cooking time.

Filling 2: Blend cream cheese, milk, sugar, egg and 1 Tbsp. flour in bowl. Pour evenly over apples. Sprinkle with crumb mixture and microwave at 100% power, uncovered for 6 - 10 minutes or until apples are tender. Rotate dish if necessary for even cooking. Serve warm or cold. May be served with whipped cream or ice cream if desired.

FRUIT CRUMBLE

1 (18½ oz.) box yellow cake mix
1 (21 oz.) can fruit pie filling mix
½ c. water

1 tsp. lemon juice
½ tsp. cinnamon

Remove 1 cup of cake mix and reserve. Sprinkle remaining dry cake mix (3 cups) in a greased 8 x 12" glass baking dish. Spread filling over cake mix. Sprinkle reserved mix over filling. Combine water and lemon and pour evenly over cake. Sprinkle with cinnamon and microwave at 100% power for 14 - 15 minutes. Rotate several times if necessary. Serve warm or cold. Great with ice cream.

FRUIT COBBLER

3 c. fresh or canned fruit
1 Tbsp. lemon juice
1⅓ c. flour
1⅓ c. brown sugar
Dash of salt

1 beaten egg and 1 Tbsp. water
8 Tbsp. melted butter
¼ tsp. ginger
½ tsp. cinnamon
½ tsp. nutmeg

Combine fruit with ⅓ cup of sugar. Cook for 1 - 2 minutes at 100% power until fruit and sugar start to form juice. Place fruit into bottom of 8 x 8" dish or equivalent round dish (preferred). Sprinkle with lemon juice. Sift dry ingredients together and toss with egg mixture, tossing with fork until crumbly. Sprinkle over fruit and drizzle with butter and cook at 70% power for 8 - 10 minutes, uncovered. If you are using a square pan you may want to "shield" the corners so they will not get overdone.

PEACH COBBLER

1½ Tbsp. arrowroot
⅓ c. brown sugar
⅓ c. water
4 c. fresh peaches, peeled,
    sliced

1 Tbsp. butter
1 Tbsp. lemon juice

Dumplings:

2 Tbsp. butter or margarine
1 egg
½ c. flour
½ c. sugar
½ tsp. baking powder
½ tsp. salt

1 tsp. cinnamon
½ tsp. nutmeg, optional
½ tsp. allspice, optional
½ Tbsp. each cinnamon and
    sugar

Mix arrowroot and sugar in round cake pan. Stir in water and add fruit, stirring gently. Microwave for 6 - 8 minutes at 100% power until thickened. Stir if necessary. Add butter and lemon juice. While peaches are cooking combine margarine for dumplings in a 1 quart container and cook at 100% for 20 seconds. Beat in egg, flour, sugar, baking powder and ½ cinnamon, allspice, nutmeg and salt. Beat until smooth. After peaches have thickened drop batter by spoonfuls in a circle over peach mixture (7 or 8 dumplings). Sprinkle with mixture of cinnamon and sugar. Cook for 10 minutes at 100% power. Spoon syrup over dumplings the last 3 minutes. Serve warm.

PEACH CRISP

Crust:

1¼ c. vanilla wafer crumbs   5 Tbsp. butter, melted

Peach Filling:

1 (9 oz.) carton frozen whipped   2 pints of fresh sliced peaches
   cream topping   (strawberries may be
1 (14 oz.) can condensed milk   substituted)
½ c. lemon juice

Melt butter in a 9 inch pie plate for 1 minute at 100% power. Stir in crumbs and press crumb mixture against bottom and sides of plate. Microwave for 2 minutes at 100% power and then chill. Blend together the whipped topping, condensed milk and lemon juice. Fold in fruit and pour into crust and chill.

BAKED CUSTARD

3 eggs, slightly beaten   1⅔ c. milk
4 Tbsp. sugar   Nutmeg
¼ tsp. salt   Cinnamon
½ tsp. vanilla   1½ c. boiling water, optional

Combine eggs, sugar, salt and vanilla in 1 quart container. Mix well. Microwave milk in a 4 cup measure for 3 minutes at 80% power. Slowly stir into the egg mixture.* If you decide to use waterbath method of cooking (this is preference only), you put the boiling water into a 2 quart casserole and place the 1 quart container of custard into this. Otherwise set custard mixture alone into oven. Cover with waxed paper and cook for 9 - 11 minutes at 50% power until custard begins to set. Center will not be firm, but will become firm when cooled. Be sure to leave covered during cooling period. * Sprinkle with cinnamon and nutmeg, if desired before cooking. This custard may be made in individual cups also. Place in circle arrangement. Cook similarly, but will take less time.

STRAWBERRIES AND CREAM TORTE

1 (11 oz.) pkg. 3 inch soft
    cookies (such as apple
    spice or oatmeal)

Strawberry Sauce:

2 c. strawberries
½ gallon ice cream (flavor of
    your choice)

3 Tbsp. sugar
2 tsp. cornstarch
½ c. pineapple or other juice

Red food coloring
1 Tbsp. brandy, optional

Line a 1½ quart souffle dish with plastic wrap, letting the plastic extend 1 to 2 inches above the dish. Gently press 7 or 8 cookies around the side of the dish, overlapping as necessary to form a scalloped edge. Place about half of the remaining cookies in bottom of dish, breaking cookies as necessary to make them fit. Stir ice cream to soft (may soften in microwave for about 1 minute at 70 - 80% power, if necessary). Spoon half of ice cream into dish. Place remaining cookies on top. Top with remaining ice cream. Cover and freeze for four hours or until firm. To serve, lift out torte by pulling up on plastic wrap. Put torte on large platter, top with berries and Strawberry Sauce (see recipe).

For sauce: Combine the sugar and cornstarch in a 1 quart measuring cup. Stir in the juice and cook in microwave for 1 - 2 minutes at 100% power until mixture bubbles. Stir and continue to cook for another minute. Remove from heat, add 3 - 4 drops of red food coloring and brandy. Cover surface with plastic wrap and cool. Pour over berries on torte to serve.

TAPIOCA PARFAITS

1 egg, separated
2 c. milk
3 Tbsp. quick cooking tapioca
5 Tbsp. sugar, divided
¼ tsp. salt

1 tsp. vanilla
¾ c. whipped cream
1½ c. fresh or frozen
    strawberries

In 1½ quart casserole blend egg yolk, milk, tapioca, 3 Tbsp. sugar and salt. Let stand 5 minutes. Beat egg white in small bowl until foamy, gradually add 2 Tbsp. sugar and continue to beat until soft peaks form. Set aside.

Stir tapioca mixture well. Microwave 80% for 5½ - 10 minutes until mixture comes to a full boil, stirring every 2 - 3 minutes. Stir in vanilla and fold in egg white. Let stand 15 minutes. Serve warm or cold if serving alone or layer cooled pudding, ¾ cup whipped cream and strawberries in parfait glasses.

notes:

Potpourri

DID YOU KNOW?

Butter can be kept firm without ice by wrapping in cloth wrung out in salt water.

Children can handle tacos, gooey sandwiches and fruit easily if they use a coffee filter instead of a napkin.

Spray recipe cards with hairspray to keep them clean.

Wash your hands in fresh lemon juice to remove onion scent.

Old powder puffs that have been cleaned in soapy water, rinsed and dried make great polishing pads for silver, copper and brass.

When doing touch up paint jobs, slip your hands into sandwich bags (for mitts) before picking up paint brush.

Plant a few sprigs of dill near your tomatoes to prevent tomato worms.

Effective insecticides for roaches and weevils is baking soda in dark cabinets and bay leaves in drawers and closets.

Marigolds prevent rodents.

Keep birds off of fruit trees by attaching plastic film to tree branches.

Ammonia sprayed into garbage sacks will prevent dogs from tearing up the bags before they are picked up.

Colored cottons that have been soaked in strong salt water overnight won't fade.

To drip-dry garments faster and with fewer wrinkles, hang them over plastic dry cleaner bags.

To prevent gravy lumps when making gravy or thickened sauces, mix flour with a bit of salted hot water before adding to sauce.

Place heel of bread on top of cabbage, broccoli or Brussels sprouts to absorb cooking odor.

Leaf lettuce dipped into soup will remove excess fat.

Mask cabbage odor by adding a few cloves in the container in which you cook it.

A pinch of soda mixed into gravy or sauce having grease on the top will cause it to mix or blend together.

Add two or three slices of raw potato and boil a few minutes to remove excess salt.

One teaspoon of sugar mixed with one tablespoon of vinegar will help remove salty taste.

Batters made with eggs and water are crisper than those made with milk.

POTPOURRI

HOME MADE BROWNING FOR MEAT

2 Tbsp. salt
2 tsp. flour

1 tsp. paprika
¼ tsp. pepper

Small amounts of spices such as chili powder, dry mustard, onion or garlic may be added to the above to suit individual tastes. Put desired spices with the above ingredients into a salt shaker and use when needed. Sprinkle a small amount of the seasoning (about ¼ tsp.) on the top of meat patty which has been slightly moistened and rub over the surface lightly to distribute evenly. This seasoning mix makes enough for 28 - 36 meat patties.

BROWNING FOR PIE CRUST AND OTHER DOUGHS

2 Tbsp. water
4 drops green food coloring

5 drops yellow food coloring
7 drops red food coloring

Mix all ingredients well. After baking the pastry apply browning with brush. Store in covered jar in refrigerator.

BECHAMEL SAUCE

2 Tbsp. butter
2 Tbsp. flour
1 Tbsp. onion, finely minced
1 c. chicken bouillon

2 tsp. heavy cream
¼ tsp. salt
Dash white pepper
Dash nutmeg

In 2 cup measure melt butter for 1 minute at 100% power. Stir in flour and onions and microwave additional 1 minute at 100% power. Add bouillon and cream. Microwave for 5 minutes at 70% power, stirring occasionally. Add seasonings at end.

EGG SAUCE

2 Tbsp. butter
2 Tbsp. flour
½ tsp. salt
½ tsp. paprika
¾ c. milk

1 (3 oz.) can mushroom buttons
1 c. (4 oz.) diced mild processed
   cheese
2 hard boiled eggs, sliced

In a 4 cup measure melt butter for 30 - 45 seconds at 100% power. Stir in flour and spices and add milk and mushrooms, including the juice. Stir all of this well and cook at 100% power for 2 - 4 minutes until the sauce boils and thickens. Remove from the oven and add the cheese. Stir until the cheese melts and sauce is smooth. Add the sliced eggs and gently fold into sauce.

Heat for 1 - 2 minutes at 50% power until heated through. This is just "super" over broccoli or cauliflower.

This recipe came from the mother of one of my students. I converted it to microwave for one lesson.

FUDGE SAUCE

2 c. brown sugar
⅔ c. light corn syrup
⅓ c. cocoa

½ c. whipping cream
¼ c. Kahlua or favorite liqueur
1 tsp. vanilla (optional)

Combine sugar, syrup, cocoa and cream. Stir until smooth. Microwave at 100% power,* uncovered, for 6 - 7 minutes until mixture boils and thickens. Stir once or twice. (This sauce does thicken while standing.) Stir in liqueur and pour into containers. Refrigerate until served, but best served warm.

*Lower temperature to 70% and cook 8 - 10 minutes if time allows. Dairy products should cook at lower temperatures for best quality.

HOLLANDAISE SAUCE

⅓ to ½ c. unsalted butter
Juice of 1 lemon

2 egg yolks

Put butter in 2 cup measure and heat 1 minute, uncovered, at 100% power. Add lemon juice and egg yolks. Beat with a small whisk for 20 seconds or until it is well mixed. Cook, 30 seconds, uncovered at 100% power. Add a dash of salt if you wish. You may reheat this, uncovered for about 40 seconds at 50% power.

HOT LEMON BUTTER

1 c. butter
Dash of salt

Juice from 2 lemons

Combine all ingredients in 2 cup container. Cover with paper towel and microwave at 100% power for 2 - 4 minutes until the butter is melted. Stir well. Sauce may be served with any food requiring butter sauce.

SAUCE IN A STICK

¾ c. butter
1½ c. nonfat dry milk
¾ c. flour

¼ c. water
1½ tsp. salt
¼ tsp. white pepper

In a 2 quart container place the butter and microwave at 50% power for 1½ to 2 minutes. Stir in powdered milk, flour, water and spices. Form into a 12 inch roll on waxed paper or plastic wrap. Wrap roll well. Store in refrigerator for up to 1 month or in the freezer for 2 - 3 months. When ready to use place ½ cup water in a 2 cup measure and microwave at 100% power for 1 - 2 minutes until boiling. Crumble 1 inch section of the stick sauce into water and stir until smooth. Microwave at 100% power for 1 - 1½ minutes until boiling. This makes ½ cup of sauce. This recipe makes 6 cups of sauce.

Variations: ½ c. cheese and dash of hot pepper with crumbled sauce = Cheese Sauce; ½ c. chicken broth for water, 1 tsp. grated onion and thyme with crumbled sauce = Bechamel; ¼ c. mayonnaise with crumbled sauce, 1 Tbsp. lemon juice, dash of hot pepper = Hollandaise.

WHITE SAUCE

2 Tbsp. butter, melted*
2 Tbsp. flour*
1 c. milk

½ tsp. salt
⅛ tsp. pepper

Microwave butter at 100% power for 30 - 50 seconds until melted. Stir in flour and seasonings. Gradually blend in milk and microwave at 50% power, stirring occasionally until thick, for 4 - 6 minutes. You may add grated cheese, if desired, for cheese sauce.

*The above recipe is for a medium white sauce. Use 1 Tbsp. butter and flour for thin; 3 Tbsp. butter and flour for thick.

DOUGH ORNAMENTS

3 c. flour
1 c. salt
1¼ c. water
Food coloring (optional)

Instant tea (optional)
¼ tsp. powdered dry alum, optional

Combine all but food coloring and tea. Tea or coloring is added to water if color is desired. Knead dough for 5 - 7 minutes. Roll out portion of dough ⅓ to ¼ inch thick on wax paper cut to fit microwave tray. Cut out 7 - 9 designs with cookie cutter and remove excess dough to save to use later. Pierce ornaments evenly with toothpick to eliminate air bubbles during cooking. Make small hole in top of ornament for hanging. Decorate with additional decorations at this point*. Slide waxed paper into microwave. Cook for 2 - 4 minutes at 100% power** or until ornaments are dry and firm. Remove from waxed paper before completely cool. *Roll out long strands of dough for use as details ... bows, facial features, etc. When ornaments are cooled, varnish or paint should be applied to seal out moisture and help preserve. **Larger pieces should be dried at 30% power at 2 minute intervals.

STRAWBERRY REFRIGERATED JAM

2 c. (1 pint) strawberries, hulled and mashed* **1½ c. sugar**
2 tsp. powdered fruit pectin**

Place strawberries in 2 quart container; next, stir in sugar and pectin. Microwave at 100% power for 3 - 4 minutes until a full rolling boil. Reduce power to 50% and cook for 5 - 6 minutes until mixture is slightly thickened. (This will also thicken as it cools.) Pour into glasses or jars and cover with plastic wrap. Store in refrigerator. *1 pkg. (10 - 12 oz.) frozen strawberries may be substituted for fresh strawberries, but you must add an additional 1 tsp. of pectin.

**For thicker jam (whether fresh or frozen strawberries are used) add additional 1 tsp. of pectin.

GARNISHES

Frosted Grapes: Paint grapes with mixture of two egg whites and 2 Tbsp. water ... then sprinkle with granulated sugar.

Lemon Basket: Cut a wedge on both sides of lemon leaving a ¼ inch "handle" in the middle of basket ... fill with parsley.

Lemon Twists: Cut lemons into ¼ inch slices. Cut through to center. Twist and tuck in a piece of parsley.

Fluted Mushrooms: Cut shallow wedges around the cap of mushroom. To help keep mushroom looking appetizingly white, boil them for 3 minutes in water with 1 Tbsp. salt and 1 Tbsp. of lemon juice.

Cucumber Cup: Cut 2" cross section from each end of cucumber. Cut thin slice off so cup will stand. Hollow out center 1½" deep. Cut ½" strips down to ¼" from bottom. Place seafood sauce in center, or cherry tomato if used for garnish only.

Radishes: Using two pencils, place radish between and slice through radish to pencil level in multiple slices, close together. Put into cold water for fanning effect. Cut off tip of radish. Cut petals starting at the stalk and make 4 cuts around base. For next layer, overlap the cuts in alternating pattern.

Lemon-Cucumber Cup: Cut lemon in half ... notch along edge. Take ¼ slices of cucumber and wedge into lemon notches. Top with small crown of parsley.

DRYING HERBS

Wash herbs and pat dry. Remove leaves from stems. Spread 1½ - 2 cups of leaves on a double thickness of paper towel. Microwave for 4 - 6 minutes at 100% power. Stir occasionally during procedure. Herbs will be brittle when dried properly. Store in air-tight container.

DRYING FRUITS AND VEGETABLES

Wash, peel (if necessary) and cut fruits or vegetables (about 1½ - 2 cups) into uniform pieces. Pat dry and spread evenly on double thickness of paper towels. Microwave at 30% power uncovered until properly dry. (1¾ - 2 hours), rearranging several times during drying period. Remove from oven; spread pieces on clean paper towel and cover with another dry paper towel. Allow to stand until pieces are thoroughly dry, showing no moisture. Store in air-tight glass container in dark area. *Sulphite crystals (1¾ tsp.) and 2 qts. of water should be used to soak apples, etc., that discolor for 15 minutes before processing.

DRYING LEAVES

Place long glass dish in oven to create a shelf effect. Next place a section of paper towel over the dish. Place a branch of three leaves (largest approximately 4 inches across) or equivalent on towel. Cover with another section of towel. Microwave for 1 - 1½ minutes at 100% power. Turn leaves over and repeat process. Time may be added or substracted according to size of leaves, etc. Do not try to dry too many leaves at once.

DRYING FLOWERS

Select a fresh flower. Select container deep enough so agent (kitty litter, borax solution or silica gel) will and can cover entire bloom (about 1 - 2 inches). Place a ½ inch layer of drying agent in container. A shoe box works well. Clip stem of flower to about ¾ - 1 inch long. Place flower in agent, face up and sprinkle more agent gently between petals of flowers making certain every petal is covered and not bent out of shape. If more than one flower is dried at a time place them so they will not touch one another. Place in oven along with a cup of water to provide moisture. Set oven about 1 - 3 minutes at 100% power depending on particular flower (see chart). After flowers have been microwaved the desired time, remove from oven. Leave in agent for 8 - 10 hours. Attach stems to wires or floral sticks. (When using silica gel the gel may begin to turn pink. Should this happen, it is losing its capability to absorb moisture. To reconstitute gel, heat in microwave a few minutes until blue color returns. You can, therefore, use the gel over and over.)

FLOWER TIME CHART

	Minutes
African Daisy	3
Aster	2½
Carnation	1
Chrysanthemum	3
Daffodil	2½
Marigold	3
Peony	3 - 4
Rose	1½
Zinnia	4 - 5

Notes:

MISCELLANEOUS INFORMATION

METRIC CONVERSION

Metric unit for volume is liters in both liquid and dry ingredients. 1000 millili-ters (ml) are in 1 liter.

When you have:	Multiply by:	Equals:
Teaspoons	5 ml	# of milliliters
Tablespoon	15 ml	# of milliliters
Dry ounces	28 ml	# of milliliters
Fluid ounces	30 ml	# of milliliters
Cups	236 ml	# of milliliters

¼ tsp. equals 1.25 milliliters
½ tsp. equals 2.5 milliliters
1 tsp. equals 5 milliliters
1 tablespoon equals 15 milliliters
¼ cup equals 0.06 liters
½ cup equals 0.12 liters
1 cup equals 0.24 liters
1 pint equals 0.48 liters
1 quart equals 0.95 liters
1 gallon equals 3.79 liters
1 ounce equals 28.00 grams
1 pound equals 0.45 kilograms

GRAMS

Metric unit for weight is grams (g) or kilograms (kg)
Kilogram = 2.2 lbs.   28 grams = 1 ounce

ounces x 28.0 = grams
pounds x .45 = kg.

CELSIUS

Metric unit for temperature is celsius. To convert fahrenheit temperature to celsius subtract 32 from fahrenheit degree and multiply by 5 and divide by 9.

Celsius to fahrenheit = celsius temperature x 9 divided by 5 add 32.

WEIGHTS & MEASURES

Dash = less than ⅛ tsp.
3 teaspoon = 1 Tablespoon
4 Tablespoon = ¼ cup
2 Tablespoon = 1 liquid ounce
8 Tablespoon = ½ cup
10 Tablespoon + 2 teaspoon = ⅔ cup
12 Tablespoon = ¾ cup
16 Tablespoon = 1 cup
8 ounce liquid = 1 cup
16 ounces = 1 pound

2 cups liquid = 1 pound
2 cup = 1 pint
4 cup = 1 quart
4 quarts = 1 gallon
8 quarts = 1 peck
4 peck = 1 bushel
1 ounce = 28.35 grams
1 gram = 0.035 ounce
1 quart = 946.4 milliliters
1 liter = 1.06 quarts

Use standard measuring spoons and cups for liquid and dry measurements. Measurements are level.

HOW MUCH AND HOW MANY!

Baking powder
  1 cup = 5½ oz.

Butter (or Margarine)
  1 stick = ½ cup
  2 cup = 1 pound

Cereals
  1 c. raw = 2 c. cooked
  4 oz. macaroni (1¼ c.) = 2¼ cooked
  4 oz. noodles (1½-2 c.) = 2 c. cooked
  7 oz. spaghetti = 4 c. cooked
  1 c. pkg. precooked rice = 2 c. cooked
  1 cup raw rice = 3-4 cups cooked

Chocolate
  1 square bitter = 1 oz.

Cocoa
  1 lb. = 4 c. ground

Cornmeal
  1 lb. = 3 c.
  1 T. = 2 T. flour

Cracker crumbs
  1½ slices bread = 1 c. soft crumbs
  1 slice bread = ¼ c. dry crumbs
  23 soda crackers = 1 c.
  15 graham crackers = 1 c.
  22 vanilla wafers = 1 c.

Cream Cheese
  1 c. whipping cream = 2 c. whipping cream

1 lb. American cheese, shredded = 4 c. or 2⅔ c. cubed
¼ lb. blue cheese, crumbled = 1 c.

Eggs
1 egg = 4 T. liquid
4-5 whole eggs = 1 c.
7-9 whites = 1 c.
12-16 yolks = 1 c.

Flour
1 lb. all-purpose = 4 c.
1 lb. cake flour = 4½ c.
1 lb. graham flour = 3½ c.

Fruits and Vegetables
Juice of 1 lemon = 3 T.
Peel of 1 lemon = 1 tsp.
5-8 medium lemons = 1 c.
Juice of 1 orange = ⅓ c.
Grated peel of 1 orange = 2 tsp.
1 medium apple, chopped = 1 c.
1 medium onion = ½ c.

Gelatin
3¼ oz. pkg. flavored = ½ c.
¼ pkg. unflavored = 1 T.

Nuts
1 lb. walnuts or pecans in shell = 1½-1¾ c. shelled
1 lb. almonds in shell = ¾ - 1 c. shelled

Shortening
1 lb. = 2 c.

Sugar
1 lb. brown = 2½ c.
1 lb. cube = 96 = 160 cubes
1 lb. granulated = 2 c.
1 lb. powdered = 3½ c.

ABBREVIATIONS

Teaspoon = tsp.
Tablespoon = Tbsp.
Cup = c.
Quart = qt.

Pint = pt.
Gallon = Gal.
Ounce = oz.
Pound = lb.

WHAT ABOUT HERBS?

All herbs and spices will keep longer if sealed tightly in a non-translucent container. Spices generally will last about six months (sometime longer) when in ground form and indefinitely if whole.

When using herbs, the conversion rule is ½ teaspoon of dried herbs equal 1 teaspoon of fresh.

TYPES OF HERBS AND FOODS THAT GO WELL

Herb	Foods They Go With	Characteristics
All Spice (whole and ground)	Fruits, meats, poultry, soups	Aromatic, spicy sweet
Basil (whole and ground)	Eggs, fish, shellfish, stuffing, and tomatoes	Delicate flavor
Bay Leaf (whole)	Tomatoes, fish, meats, sauces, soups, stuffings	Pungent flavor
Caraway (seed)	Appetizers, breads, cakes, cookies, fruit, meats	Nutty flavor
Cinnamon (stick and ground)	Beverages, desserts, fruits	Spicy, sweet aromatic
Cloves (whole and ground)	Appetizers, beverages, fruit, sauces, soups, vegetables	Spicy, sweet aromatic
Cumin (whole and ground)	Appetizers, bread, cheese, cookies, eggs, meats, pies, pilaff	Hot, spicy aromatic
Dill (seed and weed)	Fish, seafood, meat, salad	Mildly aromatic
Fennel (ground and seed)	Bread, cheese, cake, cookies, fish, seafood, fruit, meat, poultry, salads, sauerkraut	Dried fruit of parsley family
Ginger (ground and root)	Beverage, fruit, meat, soup	Warm, spicy, pungent
Marjoram (ground and whole)	Eggs, meats, poultry, salad, shellfish, stuffing, vegetables	Pungent Mint family
Nutmeg (ground)	Beverages, fruit, puddings, sauces, vegetables	Warm, spicy, pungent
Oregano (ground and leaves)	Appetizers, meats. poultry, salads, sauces, seafood, soup, vegetables	Mint family, pungent
Parsley (chopped or flakes)	Garni, garnish, sauces, salads, stews, vegetables	Light, fresh flavor

Rosemary (leaves)	Beverages, eggs, fish, meat, poultry, soups	Piney taste aromatic odor
Sage (ground)	Bread, cheese, meats, poultry, salad dressing, soups, vegetables	Mint family, slightly bitter taste
Savory (leaves)	Eggs, chicken, meats, salads, sauces, seafood, soups, stuffing	Strong, pungent aromatic
Sesame (seeds)	Bread, cake, cookies, mild cheese, garnishes, soups, vegetables	Buttery, mild
Tarragon (leaves)	Appetizers, eggs, fish, seafood, salads, sauces, soups	Strong, pungent, licorice flavor
Thyme (leaves)	Appetizers, cheese, eggs, meats, poultry, salads, seafood, soups, stuffing, vegetables	Aromatic, warm flavor

HERBS

Dry Celery tops, onion tops, and green pepper pieces in the microwave as shown in Definitive Microwave Cookery and store in freezer for use later.

CAN SIZES

Size	Wt. & Vol.	Approx, Cup Content	Chief Uses
6 oz.	6 fl. oz.	¾ cup	Frozen concentrate, natural fruits, vegetables, ripe olives
8 oz.	8 oz.	1 cup	Fruits, soups, vegetables
No. 1 (picnic)	10½ oz.	1¼ cup	
12 oz. (vacuum can)	12 oz.	1½ cup	Vacuum packed (Ex. whole grain corn)
No. 300 (1 lb. can)	14-16 oz.	1¾ cup	Pork & beans, cranberry, etc.
No. 303 16-17 oz.	16-17 oz.	2 cup	Vegetables, fruits
No. 2	1 lb. 4 oz.	2½ cup	Juices, specialties (Chinese spaghetti), few fruits & vegetables
No. 2½	1 lb. 13 oz.	3½ cup	Fruits and vegetables
46 oz. (No. 3 cylinder special)	3 lb. 3 oz.	5¾ cup	Juices, whole chicken, pork & beans, etc.
No. 10	6½-6¾ lb.	12-13 cup	Fruits, vegetables (restaurant size)

If pans are too small or large for batters of cakes recipes you make, batter can overflow, sink in middle or have coarse texture. Below is chart for adapting baking dishes from one shape and size to another.

PAN SIZE AND WHAT TO SUBSTITUTE

If recipe makes:	It will also make:
Two 9-inch layers	Two thin 8x8x2 inch squares or 18-26 2½-inch cupcakes
Three 8-inch layers	Two 9x9x2-inch squares
Two 9-inch layers	Two 8x8x2-inch squares or three thin 8-inch layers or one 15x10x1-inch rectangle or 30 2½ inch cupcakes
One 8x8x2-inch squares	One 9-inch layer
Two 8x8x2-inch squares	Two 9-inch layers or one 13x9x2-inch rectangle
One 9x9x2-inch square	Two thin 8-inch layers
Two 9x9x2-inch squares	Three 8-inch layers
One 13x9x2-inch rectangle	Two 9-inch layers or two 8x8x2-inch squares
One 12x8x2-inch rectangle	Two 8-inch layers
One 9x5x3-inch loaf	One 9x9x2-inch square or 24-30 2½-inch cupcakes
One 8x4x3-inch loaf	One 8x8x2 inch square
One 9x3½ inch tube	Two 9-inch layers or 24-32 2½-inch cupcakes
One 10x4-inch tube	Two 9x5x3-inch loaves or one 13x9x2-inch rectangle or two 15x10x1-inch rectangles

COOKING TERMS

Bake - To cook covered or uncovered in an oven-type appliance.

Baste - To moisten foods during cooking with a special sauce. Helps prevent dryness.

Beat - Whip or stir with spoon or mixer until mixture is blended with air volume.

Blanch - To precook for short time before canning or freezing.

Blend - To thoroughly mix two or more ingredients until smooth and uniform.

Boil - Cook until mixture reaches 212°. (Rolling boil means bubbles form rapidly throughout mixture.)

Braise - To cook slowly with a small amount of liquid in tightly covered pan.

Bread - Coat with crumbs before cooking.

Broil - Cook by direct heat as over coals on the barbecue.

Candied - Cooking in syrup or sugar.

Carmelize - Melting sugar slowly over low heat until it becomes brown in color.

Chill - Reducing temperature in the refrigerator.

Chop - Cutting small pieces with knife or food processor.

Cool - Removing from heat and allowing food to come to room temperature.

Cream - Beat till mixture is soft, smooth and fluffy.

Cut-in - To mix shortening and dry ingredients using pastry blender or knife.

Dice - Cut food into small uniform cubes.

Dredge - Coat with flour or other substance.

Flake - Break into small pieces.

Fold - Add ingredients gently. Use spatula to cut down through mixture; go across bottom of bowl, up and over. Stay close to surface until gently distributed.

Glaze - A mixture applied to food which adds gloss and flavor.

Grate - Using processor or grater to separate the food into fine particles.

Knead - Working dough with heel of hand with a pressing, folding motion.

Marinate - Allowing food to stand in a liquid to add flavor or to tenderize.

Mince - Finely chopping food into very small pieces.

Mix - Combining ingredients until evenly distributed.

Pit - To remove pits from fruits.

Poach - Cooking in hot liquid.

Precook - Partially cooking food before final cooking or reheating.

Roast - Cooking food, uncovered without water. (Usually in oven.)

Saute - Frying quickly. (In the microwave this can be done without liquid and covered to cause softening.)

Scald - Bring to temperature just below boiling point. (Tiny bubbles form at edge of pan.)

Scallop - Bake food with sauce or liquid. Usually crumb topped.

Score - Cut narrow slits part way through outer surface of food.

Sear - Brown surface of meat quickly with intense heat.

Shred - With shredder or processor, making small, long and narrow pieces.

Sift - Putting dry ingredients through sifter.

Simmer - Cooking in liquid at low heat (about 185°-210°).

Soft peaks - Beating egg whites or whipping cream until peaks are formed, but tips fall off.

Steam - Cook in steam. (In microwave cooking water is not needed in most cases. Necessary to cover tightly to produce steam.)

Steep - To extract flavor and color from ingredient by leaving in liquid just below the boiling point. (Such as tea.)

Stew - Simmering slowly in small amount of liquid.

Stir - Mixing ingredients in circular motion until uniformly blended.

Toss - Mixing ingredients lightly.

Truss - Securing fowl or other meat with twine, skewers, etc.

Whip - Beat rapidly to incorporate air and produce expansion. (Whip cream.)

PLANNING FOR A CROWD?

Beverages

Coffee, ground	35-40	1 pound
Cream for coffee	25	1 pint
Sugar	35	1 pound
Milk	25	1½ gallon
Tea, instant	50	1 cup
Tomato juice	50	2 No. 10 cans
Fruit juice	50	2 No. 10 cans

Desserts

Cake	24	1 15½x10½x1 inch sheet cake
Ice Cream	24	3 quarts
Pie	30	5 9-inch pies
Whipped cream	25	1 pint

Fruit

Canned	24	1 6½-7½ pound can

Meat

Beef, roast	25	12½ pounds, bone-in
Beef, ground	25	6¾ pounds
Ham, baked	25	10 pounds, boneless
Wieners	25	6 pounds
Chicken	24	6 chickens
Turkey	24	15 pounds
Turkey, roll	25	6-7 pounds
Pork, roast	25	12½ pounds

Pasta, Rice

Rice, long-grain	24	1½ pounds, uncooked
Spaghetti or noodles	25	2½ pounds, uncooked

Relishes (combine several)

Carrot strips	25	1 pound
Celery	25	3 quarts
Olives	25	1 quart
Pickles	25	1 quart

Salads

Fruit	24	2 quarts
Potato	24	3 quarts
Tossed vegetable	25	5 quarts
Slaw	25	5 quarts
Salad dressing	32	1 pint

Soup 25 1½ gallon or
10 (11 oz.) condensed

Bread
Bread 50 5 loaves
Rolls 25 50
French bread 24 1 18-inch loaf

Vegetables
Canned 24 6 1-pound cans
Baked beans 25 1½ gallons
Scalloped potatoes 25 1½ gallons
Potatoes, baked 25 9 pounds
Potatoes, mashed 24 6 pounds, raw
Lettuce, for salad, Iceberg 24 4 heads
Onions 25 6¼ pounds
Frozen vegetables 25 5-5½ pounds

Miscellaneous
Butter 35 1 pound
Catsup 35 2 14-oz. bottles
Potato chips 25 1 to 1½ pounds
Nuts 50 1½ pounds
Cheese 50 1½ pounds

EMERGENCY SUBSTITUTIONS

Baking powder plus sweet milk
Each half tsp. soda with 1 c. sour milk takes the place of 2 tsp. baking
   powder and 1 c. sweet milk.

1 c. butter or margarine = ⅞ c. lard with ½ tsp. salt. (Rendered fat is the
same ... Hydrogenated fat is 1 c. to ½ tsp. salt.)

1 c. catsup or chile sauce = 1 c. tomato sauce plus ½ c. sugar plus 2 T.
vinegar.

1 sq. (1 oz.) unsweetened chocolate = 3 T. regular type cocoa plus 1 T.
margarine or butter.

1 whole egg = 2 egg yolks or 2 T. dried whole egg with 2½ T. water.

1 clove garlic = ⅛ tsp. garlic powder.

1 T. fresh herbs = 1 tsp. dried herbs.

1 c. cake flour = 1 c. plus 2 T. all-purpose flour.

1 T. cornstarch for thickening = 2 T. flour or 4 tsp. quick cooking tapioca.

1 c. all-purpose flour = ½ bran/wheat or cornmeal plus balance of all-purpose to fill 8 oz. cup.

1 c. whole milk = ½ c. evaporated milk plus ½ c. water or 1 c. reconstituted
non-fat dry milk plus 2½ tsp. butter or margarine or 1 c. dry whole milk (4 T.
+ 1 c. milk or water).

1 c. sour milk or buttermilk = 1 T. lemon juice or vinegar plus sweet milk to
make 1 c. (let stand 5 min. or 1¾ tsp. cr. of tartar.

1 c. skim milk = 4 T. nonfat dry milk plus 1 c. water.

1 tsp. dry mustard = 1 T. prepared mustard.

1 c. tomato juice = ½ c. tomato sauce + ½ c. water.

1 c. self-rising flour = 1 c. flour, 1½ tsp. baking powder, 1 tsp. salt (sift for
less coarse texture).

Fresh basil = ¼ c. fresh parsley + 1 T. dried basil for every ¼ c. fresh
parsley.

Baking powder = 1 part baking soda + 2 parts cream of tartar + 1 part
cornstarch (does not keep well).

Nutrition is the study of what happens to food once it is ingested.

FOOD GROUPS RECOMMENDED DAILY FOR ADULTS:

Food Group	Daily Serving	Size of Serving	Principal Nutrient
Meat, Fish, Legumes Nuts and Seeds	2	2-3 oz. meat	Protein and Iron
Vegetables & Fruits	4	½ c. fruit juice 1 med. size fruit ½ c. cooked veg.; 1 c. raw veg.	Water Vitamin A Vitamin C Fiber
Bread and Cereal (Enriched or Whole Wheat)	4	½ c. cooked cereal ¾ c. ready-to-eat cereal or 1 slice bread	Thiamin Riboflavin Niacin Iron
Milk and Milk Products	2-4*	1 glass (8 oz.)	Calcium

* Calcium needs for children, teenagers and nursing women.

VITAMINS LINKED TO CANCER PREVENTION AND THEIR BEST SOURCES:

Vitamin A = Liver, eggs, cheese, butter, fortified margarine, milk, fruits and yellow-orange and dark green vegetables (carrots, broccoli, spinach, cabbage).

Vitamin C = Citrus, tomatoes, strawberries, melons, green peppers, potatoes, dark green vegetables.

Vitamin E = Vegetable oil, margarine, whole wheat grains, liver, dried beans, green leafy vegetables.

Folic Acid = Liver, dark green, leafy vegetables, wheat germ, dried beans, peas, orange juice, cantaloupe.

MEATS

Carving and Serving Tips

Standing up may make carving easier

Investigate so you will know where the bones are.

Use sharp knife.

Use simple garnish so you have space to work.

Serve on heated platter.

How to Carve

Roast Turkey and Chicken

1. Position the bird in front of you so that the legs are pointing to your right. Remove the drumstick by cutting down between the thigh and the body. With fork, push leg outward; find joint that connects thigh and back bone and cut through.
2. Remove drumstick; separate leg and thigh and carve both in uniform slices parallel to the bone. (A separate plate for this will make it easier.)
3. Make a horizontal base cut deep into the breast at point on bird where wing is attached. Find joint and remove wing.
4. Finally, place fork firmly in breast and carve thin slices, carving downward to base line made while cutting off wing. Begin slicing at a higher point on breast for each slice again cutting to baseline. Continue till breast is carved.
5. Repeat above procedure with other side of bird.

Baked Whole Ham

1. Place ham fat side up, shank to your left. Grip shank end and carve 2-3 slices from less meaty side.
2. Turn ham onto just-cut surface and cut a small wedge from shank end. Proceed slicing straight down to leg bone.
3. Release slices by cutting along leg bone away from the shank end.

OTHER CARVING INFORMATION

There are three basic directions for carving meat. They are horizontal, vertical and diagonal. The method you use depends on the cut, shape and direction of the grain. The tenderness or lack of it also help determine carving methods.

To carve meats horizontally you carve parallel to the plate or platter and the knife will never touch serving dish. No need for a cutting board.

To carve vertically you will need a carving board as you cut completely through the meat to the surface underneath.

Carving diagonally is a cross between the other two types of carving. Since each cut ends with the edge of your knife against whatever is under the meat (bone or surface), a cutting board is again used.

WHERE OUR MEAT CUTS ARE LOCATED

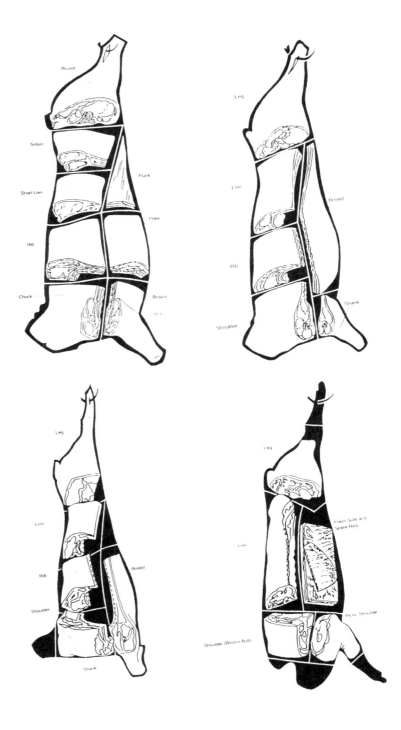

BEEF

1. *Chuck*
   Chuck Pot Roast, Arm Roast, Blade Roast

2. *Shank, Brisket, Plate*
   Corned Beef, Brisket, Short Ribs, Shanks

3. *Rib*
   Standing Rib, Rolled Rib, Ribeye Roast

4. *Short Loin*
   Top Loin, Strip Steak, Tenderloin, Rib Eye, T-Bone, Club, Porterhouse

5. *Sirloin*
   Sirloin, Boneless Sirloin

6. *Flank*
   Flank Steak, Rolled Flank, Flank Fillets

7. *Round*
   Sirloin Tip Roast, Bottom Round Steak, Round Bone, Top Round, Rolled Rump Roast, Standing Rump Roast

VEAL

1. *Shoulder*
   Shoulder and Arm Roasts, Blade Roast and Steak

2. *Shank and Breast*
   Breast, Riblets, Veal en brochette

3. *Rib*
   Rib Roast, Rib Chops

4. *Loin*
   Loin Roast, Loin Chop, Kidney Chop

5. *Leg*
   Standing Rump Roast, Rolled Rump Roast, Cutlet, Center Cut Leg Roast, Shank Half of Leg.

PORK

1. *Shoulder*
   Boston Shoulder, Smoked Shoulder Roll, Blade Steak

2. *Picnic*
   Smoked Picnic Shoulder, Canned Picnic Shoulder, Hocks

3. Loin
Crown Roast, Center Loin Roast, Rib Chop, Sirloin Roast, Tenderloin, Loin Chop, Blade Loin Roast, Back Ribs, Rib Center Chop, Canadian Bacon, Center Loin Roast Butterfly Chop

4. Fresh Side and Soare /ribs
Spareribs, Salt Side, Bacon, Slab

5. Leg
Smoked Ham, Shank, Butt, Center slice, Ham, Boneless canned Ham

LAMB

1. Shoulder and Shank, Breast
Shoulder Roast, Rolled Shoulder Roast, Saratoga Chops, Blade Chops, Arm Chops, Shanks, Riblets, Ribs, Choplets

2. Rib
Rib Roast, Rib Chops

3. Loin
Loin Roast, Loin Chop, English Chop, English Roast, Cubes for Kabobs, English Chop

4. Leg
Center Leg Roast, Leg Steak, Sirloin Chop, American, Frenched, Boneless Rolled

DID YOU KNOW?

Cooked corn beef can be flattened easily for slicing if you place weighted cutting board on top and cool in refrigerator for an hour or more before slicing. Meat can easily be reheated (50% power) in your microwave.

STORING OUR FOOD

MEAT STORAGE (Refrigerator)

BEEF

Roasts	5 to 6 days
Steaks	3-5 days
Ground beef, stew meat	2 days

PORK

Roasts	5 to 6 days
Hams, picnics, whole	7 days
Bacon	5 to 7 days
Chops, spareribs	3 days
Pork sausage	2 to 3 days

VEAL

Roasts	5 to 6 days
Chops	4 days

LAMB

Roasts	5 days
Chops	3 days
Ground lamb	2 days

POULTRY

Chickens, whole	2 to 3 days
Chicken, cut up	2 days
Turkeys, whole	4 to 5 days

COOKED MEATS

Leftover cooked meats	4 days
Cooked poultry	2 days
Ham/picnics	7 days
Frankfurters	4 to 5 days
Sliced luncheon meats	3 days
Unsliced bologna	4 to 6 days

FISH

Fresh	24 hours
Marinated	1 to 2 days

STORAGE AND BUYING GUIDE

VEGETABLE STORAGE

Type	Refrig. Time	Tips
Asparagus	4-6 days	Tips close, compact. Choose tender, firm with very little white.
Beans	2-5 days	Small seeds in pods best. Should not look dry.
Broccoli, Cauliflower Brussels Sprouts	3-7 days	Flower clusters tight and close. Sprouts firm.
Celery	7-14 days	Leaves should be green and not wilted. Rigid crisp ribs.
Cucumbers	4-5 days	Long and slender.
Mushrooms	4-5 days (brown bag in single layer)	Light in color; smooth with cap hugging stem. (At peak, most robust stage, however, cap opens)
Root vegetables (carrot, turnip, radish, beet, etc.)	4-5 days	Smooth and firm, medium size. Large can be pithy.
Peppers	4-5 days	Firm, crisp. Avoid wrinkled skin. Gloss and unblemished.

FRUIT STORAGE

Type	Ripen at Room Temp.	Refrig. Time	Tips
Apples	yes	2-4 days	Pick type that suits your need. Intense color for variety.
Berries	no	1-2 days	Plump, solid with good color. Avoid stained container indicating leakage of berries.
Cantaloupes	yes	7-10 days	Stem scar completely smooth circular indentation with no ragged edges. Yellow beneath coarse netting; fruity odor.
Watermelon	no	1 week	Deep colored rinds. Bottom that was against ground yellow rather than pale white or green.
Grapes	no	3-5 days	Firmly attached to stem.
Oranges, Grapefruit Lemons, Limes	no	10-14 days	Firm, heavy for size. Skin smooth, fine grained

Type	Will Keep	Tips
Potatoes	2 months (mature) 2 weeks (new)	Smooth, well shaped. Tight fitting skin.

FREEZER BASICS

The most effective long term frozen food storage temperature is 0° or lower.

Freezing works as a food storage method because the low temperature slows down food spoilage. Bacterial growth and enzyme action is also retarded by freezing.

TECHNIQUES FOR FREEZING

1. Freeze only top quality foods as food cannot be improved by freezing.
2. Prepare the food properly for freezing. Cleaning, blanching and cooling food are necessary for good product.
3. Package food properly. You may want food in individual portions as well as family size portions.
4. Label the packages properly. Color code packages in freezer. For example: Red for meat, green for veg, etc. You may date packages, but you might rather consider marking them with "use by" dates instead.
5. Freeze foods as rapidly as possible after preparation.
6. Use frozen foods within a reasonable length of time.

BLANCHING VEGETABLES

The microwave gives you the perfect way to blanch fresh vegetables for freezing. Microwave blanching reduces loss of vitamin C, retains color and texture of the vegetable. Blanch or cook food, covered very tightly for 3 minutes per pound. Next, place vegetables in ice water for rapid cooling and to stop the cooking process. The vegetables are then ready for packaging, cooling and freezing.

PACKAGING FOR THE FREEZER

All freezing materials should be moisture proof to hold food moisture inside and cold air outside.

Vapor proof to seal out cold air and prevent flavor and odor transfer.

Sturdy enough to hold up to stress and the shape of the food being wrapped.

STORAGE TIME FOR FROZEN FOODS

Below are suggested Maximum times for foods held at approximately 0° F.

MEATS

Beef:

Hamburger	4 months
Roasts	12 months
Steaks	12 months

Lamb:

Ground	4 months
Roasts	12 months

Pork:

Cured Pork	2 months
Fresh Pork	
Chops	4 months
Sausage	2 months
Roasts	8 months

Veal:

Chops	9 months
Cutlets	9 months
Roasts	9 months

Cooked Meat:

Meat pies, dinners, etc.	3 months

POULTRY

Chicken:

Whole	12 months
Cut-up	9 months
Livers and Gizzards	3 months

Ducks and Geese:	6 months

Turkey:

Whole	12 months
Cut-up	6 months

Cooked Chicken and Turkey:

Dinners, sliced or Pot Pies	6 months
Fried	4 months

FISH AND SHELLFISH

Fish Fillets	6 months
Fish Steaks (such as salmon)	2 months
Fish, whole	3-4 months

Shellfish:

Shrimp	12 months

Clams and Dungeness Crab	3 months
King Crab	9-10 months
Shucked Oysters	3-4 months
Cooked fish and shellfish	2-3 months

VEGETABLES AND FRUITS

Fruits and Juice Concentrates	12 months
Vegetables	8 months

BAKED GOODS

Breads and Rolls	2-3 months
Sweet rolls, doughnuts, Danish	2-3 months
Cakes:	
Angel and Chiffon	2 months
Pound, Layer	4-6 months
Pies (unbaked)	8 months
Pies (baked)	6 months

OTHER FREEZER FACTS AND TIPS

Vitamin C content of broccoli, cauliflower, peaches and spinach may be reduced to half when these foods are frozen for several months. Peas and asparagus on the other hand retain most of their vitamin C for a year or longer. Therefore, it is wise to use freezer vegetables as quickly as possible.

Place vegetable and meat juices in ice cube trays; freeze and store for later use. Great for adding to soups, stocks, etc.

Place unused tomato paste by the tablespoon (9 T. per small can) on waxed paper. Freeze and transfer into storage container for use later.

Pack fruits and vegetables flat in freezerbags before you freeze them; file them upright in large shoe box to utilize your space. Loose items won't come crashing out of the freezer.

EGGS IN THE FREEZER:

Freeze egg white in ice cube trays. 1 cube = approximately 1 T. or the equivalent of 1 egg white. Store in air tight container.

Whole and yolks must be stabilized before freezing. Break yolks and blend in ⅛ tsp. (for savory dishes) and 1½ tsp. (for sweet dishes) of sugar or corn syrup per 2 whole eggs or 4 egg yolks. Then freeze in ice cube trays and transfer to air tight container. These will keep for up to 1 year.

NUTRITION

FRUITS AND VEGETABLES

Washing - Scrubbing vigorously can destroy vitamins and minerals. Rinse fresh fruits and vegetables quickly. Rub gently if dirty, but never soak.

Cutting
Wait till the last possible moment to slice fresh vegetables and fruit because cutting and tearing destroy vitamin C.

Cooking
Produce has the most food value when it is eaten raw. To minimize loss of nutrients use as little water as possible to cook. Therefore, microwave oven cooking is an excellent way to preserve minerals and vitamins because no water or very little is used.

Deep fat frying can destroy nutrients and boiling is least healthful.

MEATS AND POULTRY

Stewing and braising can destroy important vitamin B. Faster methods such as microwave cooking, broiling, frying help to lock in vitamins.

Rare steak, therefore, will contain more nutrients than a well done one simply because it has been exposed to high heat for less time.

Barbecuing reduces fat content, but microwaving reduces fat content even more quickly as the microwaves are attracted to the fat content of the food before the water content. The microwave effectively cooks out excess fat more quickly than other methods.

Other Nutritional factors

Refrigeration of fresh peas and lima beans in their pods help maintain nutritional value.

Rinsing rice or pasta after cooking causes vitamin loss.

Cooking pasta in salt water may draw out valuable vitamins.

When refrigerating, remember the shorter the storage time and the cooler the temperature, the less vitamins and minerals are lost.

Milk and cream retain more nutrients longer when stored in opaque containers.

More About Nutrition and Diet

Microwave off fat in a flash. It is possible to cook out a good amount of fat in foods because microwaves are attracted to fat molecules. Fat cooks faster than the water content of food. Therefore, fat melts away before food becomes too done.

Vegetables and fruits are more nutritious in the microwave because no water or very little is added. Vitamins and minerals, therefore, are not leached out as they are when cooked conventionally.

Example: In a Vit. C study 3½ oz. of microwaved cabbage emerged with 43 mg. of Vit. C. versus 25 mg. of Vit. C for stove cooked.

Although grains don't necessarily cook quicker than conventionally, grains are microwave stars as they become plumper and fluffier.

EXERCISE AND DIET

Working up to exercising beyond 30 minutes allows the body to burn more fat or calories so if it is weight loss you are after, consider increasing the duration of your aerobic activity beyond 30 minutes.

Whatever the activity, exercise until your heart reaches a Target Heart Rate (THR) of 70-85% of your Maximum Heart Rate (MHR) according to your age. To determine this follow this formula:

$$MHR = 220 - age$$
$$THR = MHR \times 70\% \text{ to } 85\%$$

During exercising, your heart rate per minute should remain within the target zone. Always check with your physician before starting an exercise program to determine your training goals.

Check your pulse beats during a 10 second period and multiply this by 6 to determine whether you are within your THR. Do this every 10 minutes until you learn to judge your THR. After you can do this for a time, check only halfway through workout and immediately afterwards. This workout should be done 3 or 4 times a week to keep yourself fit. Always, however, remember to ease into and out of your workout with a warm-up and cool-down.

ABOUT CHOLESTEROL

Cholesterol is a fat-like substance found in all foods of animal origin such as meat, dairy, but not in foods from plants. Some cholesterol is needed by the body, but too much can build up in arteries and cause heart disease, etc.

Be sure to check food labels so that hidden fats and cholesterol such as egg yolk solids, lard, whole-milk products do not cause "cholesterol free" vegetable products such as coconut and palm oils and other foods to be more saturated.

Good nutrition means a "balance" of the nutrients .....
Combine food groups and servings in proper amounts so that you will get the benefits from your foods. Too much of anything, even "healthy" food is not good. Proper balance is the answer to good nutrition.

Even when counting calories keep all food groups in your basic diet every day.

HINTS FOR DIETERS

Lighten your coffee with skim-milk rather than coffee whitener.

Want to lose five pounds painlessly? Eliminate one teaspoon of butter or margarine a day. You will save over 16,000 calories a year (equal to about 5 pounds as it takes 3,500 calories to make one pound).

Choose diet margarine instead of butter or regular margarine.

Honey and maple syrup have more calories than sugar ... Go easy!

Foods that need a lot of chewing such as raw vegetables and grainy breads are more satisfying and help you eat less ... gives your brain time to give you the message you are full.

Always stop eating when full.

No caloric way to zest a salad (as the dressings are what add the calories) is to sprinkle a little garlic salt over greens ... can add lemon or lime juice, too.

PIECRUSTS THE MICROWAVE WAY

No-Roll Pie Shell

1 cup flour
¼ cup confectioners' sugar
½ cup soft butter or margarine
¼ cup finely chopped pecans
⅛ teaspoon salt

Mix the ingredients together to form a soft ball and press firmly in bottom and sides of 9-inch pie plate. Do not press on rim. Microwave at 70% power for 7 to 9 minutes.

Easy Piecrust

½ cup salad oil
1 T. butter or margarine
¼ cup milk or water
½ tsp. salt
1½ cups flour
5 or 6 drops yellow food coloring
   or browning drops on page 117

Combine ingredients in mixing bowl and stir. Press dough out and up sides of pie pan to form shell. This pie crust can be shaped over rim so you may dampen with water around the edges to help it adhere to the pan. Microwave at 70-80% power for 7-9 minutes. Turn if necessary for even cooking.

Oatmeal Piecrust

½ c. one-minute oatmeal
¼ c. flour
½ c. margarine
2 T. sugar
½ c. chopped nuts

Combine ingredients. Mix well to form soft dough. Press firmly into greased 9-inch pie pan. Bake in microwave at 70-80% power for 7-9 minutes, turning when needed.

FACTS ABOUT MICROWAVING PIECRUST

Pie crust should always be pre-cooked in the microwave. Crusts will be very flaky although they do not brown. Spices or the browning drops on page 117 of Definitive Microwave Cookery may be added for coloring.

For two crust pies, microwave crust separately; then assemble and microwave again.

Frozen pie shells may be removed from container and placed over the bottom of pie dish and microwaved. This will prevent poorly shaped or warped bottoms. They may also be placed loosely in plate and pricked on bottoms and sides. After cooking, rotating when necessary, a mixture of egg and water may be brushed on and cooked another minute to seal the holes.

TIPS

If bottom of pastry is not cooking dry, elevate pie plate on overturned saucer or casserole cover.

A pie crust is easier to make if all the ingredients are cool.

Egg whites for meringue should be room temperature before beating for greater volume.

For unusually fluffy meringue you may add ¼ tsp. vinegar to egg whites.

Meringue will not shrink if you spread it on the pie so it touches the crust on each side before you bake it.

Substitute crushed cornflakes in a pecan pie if you don't have any nuts. They will rise to the top like nuts and give a great, crunch flavor.

Sprinkle pie crust with powdered sugar to prevent crust from becoming soggy with cream pie.

Put a layer of marshmallows in the bottom of a pumpkin pie before you add the filling and the marshmallows will become the topping as they rise to the top.

A teaspoon of vinegar added to pecan pie syrup will cut the sugary sweetness and bring out the flavor.

DECORATIVE PIE CRUSTS

Pinched edge: Works well with single crust. With index finger on the inside of pastry rim and the other index finger and thumb on the outside, pinch the crust into V-shaped ridges.

Rope edge: This works well on double or single crust. Pinch the top and bottom crust together between your thumb and index finger at an angle to the rim. Ridges resemble the parallel strands of a rope.

WHAT ABOUT THOSE STAINS! ! ! ! !

Alcoholic Beverages
Pre-soak fresh stains with club soda or cold water; then glycerine and cold water. Stain should then be rinsed with vinegar. If wine stains remain you may rub in concentrated detergent and wait 15-20 minutes. Rinse. Repeat above if necessary. Wash article with detergent in the hottest water safe for the fabric. For wine, sprinkle table salt on stain to absorb it. When salt dries, brush off.

Animal Stains
Sponge with cold water and spray mixture with three tablespoons of white vinegar to one quart water. Sponge with detergent suds and rinse.

Blood
Soak in cold water and non-chlorine bleach if fabric is washable. When spot is removed, wash garment in hot water and detergent. If non-washable, sponge with a solution of 1 ounce household ammonia mixed with 10 ounces of water before sending to cleaners.

Candle Wax
Scrape off cold wax with knife. Press spot between paper towels and sponge with a dry-cleaning fluid before washing in hot water and detergent. Or scrape surface wax off with dull knife, then place stain between clean white paper towels and press with warm iron. If stains remain apply a cleaning solution and blot with more paper toweling. After dry, launder cloth, using chlorine bleach if cloth will take it.

Chewing Gum
Rub gum with ice cube to chill and harden for easier removal. Next, scrape off as much as possible with a knife. Sponge with mineral spirits and air dry. Wash as usual.

Cigarette Burns (to rugs)
Clip off blackened ends, work in detergent solution and rinse well.

Chocolate and cocoa
Prewash by soaking in warm water and detergent. When stain is removed, wash in hot water, detergent and bleach.

Coffee
Rub garment with a yellow, heavy-duty laundry soap and soak in cold water for several hours. Before washing, scrub stain again thoroughly. If stain still remains, continue to rub with soap and soak until stain is gone. Wash in hot water and detergent.

Crayons
Rub liquid detergent or paste from powdered detergent and water directly on stain. Allow to stand overnight. Wash in hot water and detergent. Baking powder added to wash water also helps.

Ball Point Pen
Try one of the following or all: Dry-Cleaning fluid, rubbing alcohol or hairspray. Still not out, pour denatured alcohol through the stain, but in petroleum jelly and sponge with cleaning solvent. The garment may then be soaked in detergent and later washed in detergent and bleach safe for fabric.

Soft Drinks
Soak in cold water with mild liquid detergent and 1 T. white vinegar for 15 minutes. Rinse in clear water. If stain still remains, sponge with rubbing alcohol and wash. Still remains ... 1 quart warm water and 1 T. of enzyme pre-soak product for 30 minutes should do the trick.

Egg
Scrape with knife to remove all you can. Soak in cold water and detergent or enzyme pre-soak product. When stain is removed, wash in detergent and hot water.

Fruit and Juices
Soak in 1 qt. warm water with about ¼ tsp. mild liquid detergent, and 1 T. white vinegar for about 15 minutes. Rinse with clear water. If the stain is still there sponge with rubbing alcohol and wash. Still there? 1 T. enzyme pre-soak and a quart of warm water should do it.

Milk and Cream
Pre-treat in cold water with detergent. When spot is removed wash in hot water and detergent. Grease spots should be sponged with non-flammable dry cleaning detergent and washed again.

Meat Juice
Blot juice and remove any traces of food. Pre-soak 30 min. cold water. Sponge with cold water and a non-chlorine bleach.

Gravy, Grease or Oil
Pre-treat with liquid detergent or liquid enzyme product. Let stand several hours and wash in hot water and detergent.

Paint
(Scrape off all excess paint.)
Water-base ... Pretreat in cold water and detergent. When spot is removed, wash in hot water and detergent.
Oil-based ... Soak in turpentine for 30 minutes. Rinse out and air dry. After dry, rub detergent into stain and soak in hot water for another hour. When stain is removed, wash as usual.

Grass
Treat with liquid detergent or paste made from dry detergent and water. Let stand several hours and wash in hot water and detergent.

Grease, Gravy, Oil, Tar
Remove as much of grease with powder. Pretreat with detergent or liquid enzyme product. Let stand several hours and wash with lots of detergent or rub the spot

with lard and sponge with dry cleaning solvent. Follow by washing in hot water.

Rust
Wet rust stains and rub in bathroom cleanser containing oxalic acid. Leave on for 30 minutes before washing. Repeat if necessary. Tomato juice is also very effective in removing spots on either clothes or hands. Rinse thoroughly with warm water afterward.

Nail Polish
Scrub with fingernail polish remover. When stain is removed, wash as usual. If stain is still there, sponge with denatured alcohol and a few drops of ammonia. Wash again.

Deodorants
Sponge area with white vinegar. If this does not remove the stain, soak in denatured alcohol and wash with detergent and hot water.

Mildew
Remove with a solution of chlorine bleach and water (½ to 1 cup of bleach to 1 gal. water). Fabric can be saturated with lemon juice, rubbed with salt and placed in the sun for several hours.

Dye
When dye transfers during washing, immediately bleach discolored items, before drying. Whites must be treated with color remover.

Tea
Soak in cold water. Wash with detergent and bleach safe for fabric.

Scorch
Wash with detergent and bleach safe for the fabric. If stain is quite heavy, cover the stain with a cloth dampened with hydrogen peroxide. Cover with dry cloth and press with hot iron. Rinse well. Remember, severe scorching cannot be removed.

Carpet
Instant spot removers for carpets can be one of the following: Prewash commercial sprays, glass cleaner, club soda, shaving cream, or toothpaste. Simply rub it in and wait a few minutes before sponging off thoroughly. If the stain remains, combine two tablespoons of detergent, four tablespoons of white distilled vinegar and one quart of warm water. Work into stain and blot well.

Felt Markers
Spray with hairspray and wipe.

Lipstick
Treat with yellow laundry soap on spot. Soak in cold water overnight. Rub more soap onto lipstick and wash as usual. Repeat if necessary.

OTHER CLEANING AND STAIN TIPS

Water in which potatoes have cooked will clean egg blackened silverware. Soak silver in still warm water for a couple of minutes, rinse in hot water. Dry and polish.

If soap film on your glass shower doors is a problem, wipe them clean with any furniture polish that has lemon oil base. If film is especially heavy, use steel wool pad soaked in a dishwashing liquid. The glass will sparkle.

Try using some regular laundry bleach on vinyl floor stains ... might just come out.

Has the procelain on your sink or toilet lost its shine? Wash it in mild solution of vinegar and water, applied with a soft rag. This should restore the shine.

Toilet bowl stains can be removed by washing them with regular bleach. If you can't get the stains this way, soak paper towels in bleach and plaster them over the stains for an hour or two. Scrub and rinse.

When glass jars become splattered with corn or vegetable oil, get rid of that stickiness by using more of the same oil.

Vinegar water solution will prevent mold from forming in lunch and bread boxes.

Raw potato rubbed over hands will remove vegetable stains.

Remove coffee or mineral stains from glass pot with lemon slice.

Clean cement with straight bleach and a stiff bristled brush.

Small garden tools store well and don't rust when you stand them up in a pail filled with sand mixed with a bit of oil.

Clean rusted garden tools with cork dipped in scouring cleanser.

FIRST AID GENERAL DIRECTIONS

Rescue as quickly as possible.
Make certain airway is open.
Control severe bleeding by direct pressure.
Do not move the victim unless altogether necessary.
Keep patient from becoming chilled.
Try to determine injuries or why patient has become ill.
Call for help if necessary, otherwise carry out the indicated first aid.

THE NEW LIFESAVERS

Heart Attack

Unlike heartburn or muscle spasm, in a heart attack the pain feels as if the chest is being squeezed. Most describe it by making a fist over the breastbone. Other symptoms include troubled breathing, palpitations and "a racing heart."

What to do if you suspect a person of having an attack

Victim should lie down.
Call for help.
If victim loses consciousness, start CPR if you know how.

CPR (Cardiopulmonary Resuscitation)
A. Airway
Tilt victim's head as shown in A. (This alone could start breathing.) Look and listen for breathing. Look at chest to see if it is moving. If there are no signs of breathing start ...

B. Breathing
Pinch victim's nostrils closed.
Take a deep breath and seal his mouth with yours.
Blow into his mouth 4 times.
With 2 fingers on either side of the Adam's apple, check the carotid for pulse.

C. Circulation (if no response)
Kneel at victim's side.
Place both hands (one on top of other) on lower half of breastbone.
Start pressing down hard with the weight of your body at the rate of 80 times per minute. (Breast should be depressed 1½" each time.)
Do this 15 times.
Next, tilt head back and give victim 2 breaths.
Maintain 15- and 2- rhythm until he regains consciousness or help arrives.

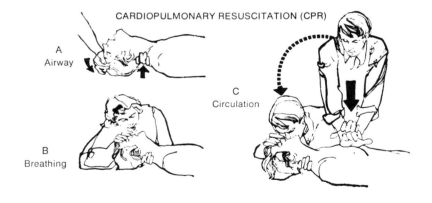

CARDIOPULMONARY RESUSCITATION (CPR)

A
Airway

C
Circulation

B
Breathing

Insect Stings
If someone stung starts to feel breathing difficulties or tightness in chest, get him to an emergency room immediately. If unconscious, call an ambulance and start CPR.

Drowning
If awake in water, reach for victim with a pole or rope if available. If person loses consciousness swim to drowning person, grab hair and pull him with head above water to shore. If not breathing, start CPR.

Poisoning
If a poisonous substance is swallowed, breathed in or spilled on eyes and skin, follow these procedures and call your poison information center for further advice.

Swallowed:
If awake give him a glass of water. Take the poison container to telephone when calling center. Everyone should have a one-ounce bottle of syrup of ipecac in the medicine cabinet as it is frequently recommended. Ipecac causes the poison to be vomited, but always check with your poison center first.

Never make a patient vomit if he is having fits, has swallowed a corrosive such as lye, or a poison such as lighter fluid, furniture polish, etc. Give liquids instead. A mixture of water and lemon juice or vinegar followed by milk is recommended. Keep patient warm and lying down.

Inhaled:
Ventilate area and carry victim to fresh air.

In the eyes:
Hold the victim's eyelid open and flush out with tepid water for 10-15 min.

On the Skin:
Wash area with clear water. Remove contaminated clothing.

Shock:
Keep victim lying down, head lower than body. Never give liquid when person is unconscious. Keep victim warm, but not hot. Of course, call for help immediately. Shock is a disturbance in the balance between blood vessels and nervous system and can cause unconsciousness or coma if not treated.

Burns:
Apply burned area with cold water. Do not apply grease or ointment. Call a doctor and keep patient warm, but not hot until help arrives.

Heat Exhaustion:
Similar symptoms as shock ... clammy, pale, weak pulse ... victim is usually conscious. Keep him lying down, legs elevated and wrap him in a blanket. Give him salt water (1 tsp. salt to 1 glass water). Every 15 minutes administer ½ glass. Call the doctor.

Choking:

The universal distress signal for choking is the victim clutching his neck with one hand. He cannot talk or breathe. Don't try to remove the food, you may push it deeper. Act immediately as a choking victim has only 4 minutes to live! Follow as shown to perform the Heimlich Maneuver.

- If no help is at hand, victim should try to perform Heimlich Maneuver on himself by pressing his own first upward into the abdomen and backing himself forcefully against a wall.

- It is important for victim to see a doctor immediately after that to make sure that an injury was not caused by the maneuver which saved his life.

- Small children should be held upside down and slapped fairly hard between the shoulder blades until the object is expelled.

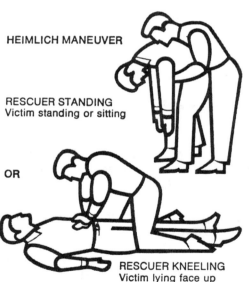

HEIMLICH MANEUVER

RESCUER STANDING
Victim standing or sitting

OR

RESCUER KNEELING
Victim lying face up

- Stand behind victim and wrap your arms around his waist.
- Grasp your fist with other hand and place fist against victim's abdomen, slightly above the navel and below the rib cage.
- Press your fist into victim's abdomen with a **quick upward thrust.**
- Repeat several times if necessary.

When victim is sitting, rescuer stands behind victim's chair and performs maneuver in same manner.

- Victim is lying on his back.
- Facing victim, kneel astride his hips.
- With one of your hands on top of the other, place the heel of your bottom hand on the abdomen slightly above the navel and below the rib cage.
- Press into the victim's abdomen with **a quick upward thrust.**
- Repeat several times if necessary.

My father said he always felt closest to God when he was out in nature ... Below is a poem he wrote one day while he was fishing.

POEM BY GRANDPA "SCOTTIE"
(Father of Carolyn Dodson)

Go to God's river and see the trees ...
Hear the song of birds and bees.

Go to God's river, cast in your bait ...
forget man and all his hate.

Go to God's river cast aside your work ...
fish in deep water where lumbers lurk.

Go to God's river and feel the breeze ...
as He stirs it for you to appease.

Go to God's river where fishes hide ...
talk with Him there by your side.

Go to God's river cut through the sand ...
by years of toil made by His hand.

Go to God's river hang on to your pole ...
throw off the sins and save your soul.

Go to God's river, sit by His pool ...
there we learn the Golden Rule.

HOW TO RAISE A JUVENILE DELINQUENT

1. Begin at infancy to give the child everything he wants. In this way he will grow up to believe the world owes him a living.
2. When he picks up bad words, laugh at him. This will make him think he's cute.
3. Never give him any spiritual training. Wait until he is 21 and then let him decide.
4. Pick up everything he leaves lying around, books, shoes, etc. Do everything for him so that he will be experienced in throwing all responsibility on others.
5. Quarrel frequently in his presence. In this way he will not be too shocked when the home is broken later.
6. Give a child all the spending money he wants. Never let him earn his own. Why should he have things as tough as you had them?
7. Satisfy his every craving for food, drink and comfort. Denial may lead to harmful frustration.
8. Take his part against neighbors, teachers, policemen. They are all prejudiced against your child.
9. When he gets into real trouble, apologize for yourself by saying, "I never could do anything with him."
10. Prepare for life of grief. You are bound to have it ... and how!

Provided through the courtesy of the Houston Police Department

INDEX OF RECIPES

APPETIZERS

ARTICHOKE DIP 1
BROCCOLI CHEESE DIP.................... 1
CHILI CON QUESO........................ 1
CHILI DIP 2
CHIMALE DIP............................. 2
MEXICO CITY DIP......................... 2
HOT CLAM DIP 3
PIZZA FONDUE 3
MEXICAN CHICKEN 3
CHICKEN LIVER RUMAKI 4
VEGETABLE RUMAKI 4
FRANK KABOBS 5
MEATBALLS DELUXE...................... 5
MEATBALLS AND SWEET/SOUR
    SAUCE.............................. 5
MUSHROOMS IN GARLIC BUTTER.......... 6
STUFFED MUSHROOMS 6
GARLIC SHRIMP.......................... 7
TORTILLAS IN CHILI SAUCE.............. 7
SHRIMP APPETIZER TREE................. 7
HOT HERBED PRETZELS 8

EGGS, CHEESE, GRAIN AND PASTA

EGGS - CHEESE
BAKED EGGS 9
FRIED EGGS 9
"MICROWAVE" HARD-BOILED EGGS 9
POACHED EGGS........................... 9
SCRAMBLED EGGS 10
BREAKFAST ON A BUN.................... 10
EGGS BENEDICT 10
FRAMED EGG 11
SPECIAL SCRAMBLED EGGS.............. 11
EGGS DELISH 11
BASIC OMELET........................... 12
DUTCH OMELET.......................... 12
MEXICAN OMELET ROLL 12
FARM COUNTRY EGGS.................... 13
BACON AND CHEESE CASSEROLE 13
ENCHILADAS MONTEREY................. 14
QUICHE DELUXE 14
QUICHE WITH HASH BROWN POTATO
    CRUST.............................. 15
BROCCOLI-RICE QUICHE 15
SAUSAGE STRATA 16

BREADS
GARLIC BREAD........................... 17
PULL APART BACON BREAD.............. 17
SAVORY CHEESE BREAD................. 17
SWEET CHERRY NUT BREAD............. 18
SOUR CREAM COFFEECAKE.............. 18
MEXICAN CORN BREAD 19
UPSIDE DOWN BRUNCH CAKE............ 19
MUFFINS ALL GONE 20
CARAMEL NUT ROLL..................... 20

GRAINS AND PASTA
CHEESE GRITS........................... 21
GREEN RICE 21
HERBED RICE 22
MACARONI AND CHEESE................. 22
NOODLE PUDDING....................... 22
VEGETABLE FETTUCCINI 23
PASTA PRIMAVERA....................... 23

MEXICAN LASAGNA...................... 24
ONE STEP LASAGNE..................... 24
GREEN NOODLES WITH RICH MEAT
    SAUCE.............................. 25
EASIER THAN LASAGNE CASSEROLE...... 25
BEEF TETRAZZINI 25
CHART FOR COOKING CEREAL 27
CHART FOR COOKING RICE AND
    OTHER GRAINS....................... 28
CHART FOR COOKING PASTA............. 29

SOUPS, SALADS AND SANDWICHES

SOUPS
CREAM OF BROCCOLI SOUP 31
QUICK AND EASY CLAM CHOWDER 31
OLIVE CARROT CREAM SOUP 32
MEXICAN CHEESE SOUP................. 32
TORTILLA SOUP 32

SALADS
GOURMET ASPARAGUS SALAD 33
AVOCADO SALAD WITH GRAPEFRUIT
    AND BACON.......................... 33
GAZPACHO SALAD....................... 33
GOLD DOLLAR SALAD 34
SPINACH SALAD......................... 34
SPINACH SALAD WONDERFUL 35
DIVINE VEGETABLE SALAD 35
PRETZEL SALAD......................... 35
SHERBET SALAD 36
PASTA-SALMON SALAD 36
RICE SALAD 37
CHICKEN SALAD......................... 37
CHICKEN SALAD A LA ORANGE.......... 37
PINEAPPLE FILLED WITH FRUITED
    CHICKEN............................ 38
TACO SALAD 38
CHICKEN CHEDDAR SANDWICH.......... 39

SANDWICHES
CHEESE FRANKS......................... 40
MUNCH POCKET SANDWICHES 40
SLOPPY JOES............................ 40

FRUITS AND VEGETABLES

FRUITS
BAKED APPLE OR PEAR 41
BING CHERRY COMPOTE 41
CRANBERRY SAUCE 41
FRUIT COMPOTE 41
CURRIED FRUIT 42
HOT MUSTARD PEACHES................. 42

VEGETABLES
ARTICHOKES WITH SOUR CREAM
    AND HORSERADISH SAUCE............ 43
ASPARAGUS SPEARS WITH WINE
    BUTTER 43
BROCCOLI ALMONDINE WITH HOT
    POPPY SEED SAUCE.................. 43
BROCCOLI CASSEROLE 44
BROCCOLI STUFFED TOMATOES 44
BRUSSELS SPROUTS CASSEROLE 45
CARROTS AU GRATIN 45

A

FROSTED CAULIFLOWER.................. 46
SCALLOPED EGGPLANT.................. 46
LIMA BEANS AND BROCCOLI
   CASSEROLE.......................... 46
BAKED POTATO......................... 47
MISSION POTATOES..................... 47
FABULOUS STUFFED POTATOES........... 48
OVEN BROWNED POTATOES.............. 48
SCALLOPED "RED" POTATOES........... 49
HAWAIIAN SWEET POTATOES............ 49
SPINACH AND ARTICHOKE HEARTS....... 49
SPINACH WITH GARLIC 50
ACORN SQUASH WITH APPLE AND
   RAISIN GLAZE....................... 50
"MORELLE" SQUASH 50
SPAGHETTI SQUASH WITH TOMATO
   SAUCE.............................. 51
OLD ITALY TOMATOES 51
SPICY CREAMED TURNIPS 52
VEGETABLES EXTRAVAGANZA............ 52
VEGETABLE MEDLEY..................... 53
ZUCCHINI SOUFFLE..................... 53
ZUCCHINI AND TOMATOES............... 53

ENTREES

BASIC PRECEPTS OF MEAT COOKERY..... 55
TENDER CUTS 55
LESS TENDER CUTS..................... 55
RELATING MICROWAVE COOKING
   TEMPERATURES TO CONVENTIONAL
   COOKING TEMPERATURES.............. 55
LOWERING COOKING TEMPERATURES..... 56
VARIOUS DEGREES OF DONENESS 56
STANDING TIME 57

BEEF
MEAL IN DISH VARIATION................ 57
MARINATED KABOBS..................... 58
HAMBURGER PATTIES................... 58
HAMBURGER TOPPINGS.................. 58
LAYERED MEAT LOAF 59
BACON WRAPPED MINI LOAVES 60
ROLLED MEATLOAF...................... 60
BEEF WITH BROCCOLI 61
BROILED STEAK A LA MICROWAVE........ 61
GRILLED STEAK SOUTHWESTERN......... 61
BEEF TENDERLOIN 62
BRISKET............................... 63
LAZY DAY POT ROAST 63
IMPOSSIBLE CHEESEBURGER PIE......... 64
CHILI WEEKEND CONCOCTION............ 64
EGGPLANT MOUSSAKA 64
REUBEN IN A CASSEROLE 65
ELEGANT STEAK AND RICE 65
STUFFED PEPPERS...................... 66

LAMB
LEG OF LAMB........................... 67

PORK
SAUSAGE STUFFED EGGPLANT........... 68
ZUCCHINI MEAT BOATS 68
GLAZED HAM 68
HAM AND BROCCOLI CASSEROLE 69
BAR B Q RIBS WITH SAUERKRAUT........ 69
SAVORY PORK CHOPS 70
PORK CHOPS WITH APPLE DRESSING..... 70
PORK CHOPS AVEC ONION............... 71
PORK CHOPS WITH PEAS AND
   CREAMY RICE........................ 71

PORK CHOPS WITH SAUERKRAUT
   AND BEER 71
PORK STUFFED TURNIPS 72
ROAST LOIN OF PORK WITH APRICOT
   GLAZE.............................. 72
FRUITED PORK ROAST................... 73

POULTRY
CHICKEN MEAL IN A DISH VARIATION 74
FRIED CHICKEN 74
FABULOUS CHICKEN CASSEROLE........ 75
CHICKEN CHASSEUR 75
CHICKEN DIJONNAIS.................... 76
CHICKEN STUFFED WITH ASPARAGUS..... 76
CHICKEN BREASTS STUFFED WITH
   CRAB MEAT 77
CHICKEN WITH SHERRIED CHEESE
   SAUCE.............................. 77
GOURMET CHICKEN BREASTS............ 78
CHICKEN WITH FRESH MUSHROOM
   STUFFING........................... 78
CHICKEN PARMESAN 79
STUFFED CHICKEN THIGHS 79
CHICKEN TERIYAKI 80
CHICKEN ARTICHOKE "DELUXE".......... 80
CHICKEN OR TURKEY ENCHILADAS
   CASSEROLE......................... 81
CHICKEN MONTEREY 81
TORTILLAS WITH CHICKEN 82
CHICKEN SPAGHETTI 82
ROAST TURKEY 83
TURKEY ROLL UP 83
TURKEY ENCHILADAS................... 84

VEAL
VEAL PARMIGIANA 85

FISH AND SEAFOOD
BAKED FISH FILLETS 86
GOLDEN FISH FILLETS.................. 86
RED SNAPPER FILLETS WITH
   ARTICHOKES 86
CRAB BAKED AVOCADOS................. 87
CRAB ENCHILADAS..................... 87
LOBSTER TAILS 88
AVOCADO AND SCALLOPS DIVINE......... 88
SHRIMP CASSEROLE.................... 89
SHRIMP GUMBO........................ 89
STEAMED SHRIMP...................... 90

DESSERTS AND SWEETS

BARS AND COOKIES
FIRST PRIZE BROWNIES 91
FRUIT CHEWY BROWNIES................ 91
BROWNIE PIE 91
CHOCOLATE CHIP COOKIES 92
CHOCOLATE CHIP SQUARES............. 92
CHOCOLATE CHIP MARBLE BARS 93
CHOCOLATE/SCOTCH BARS 93
CRAZY COOKIES 93
CREME DE MENTHE BARS 94
LEMON CHEESECAKE BARS 94
MARSHMALLOW-BUTTERSCOTCH
   BARS.............................. 95
NUT SQUARES 95
CRUNCHY PEANUT BARS 96
TOFFEE GRAHAMS...................... 96

B

CAKES AND FROSTINGS
AMARETTO BUNDT CAKE 97
APPLE FLAMBE 97
APRICOT CRUMBLE 98
BUTTER CROWN POUND CAKE 98
CARROT CAKE 99
AMARETTO SWIRL CHEESECAKE 99
PRALINE CHEESECAKE 100
CHERRY NUT CAKE 100
SELF-ICING CHOCOLATE CAKE 101
CRANBERRY CAKE WITH BUTTER
   RUM SAUCE 101
GINGERBREAD WITH LEMON BUTTER
   SAUCE 102
ICE CREAM CONE CUPCAKES 102
OATMEAL CAKE 103
DEEP DISH PINEAPPLE CRUMBLE 103
SNICKER CAKE 103
STRAWBERRY CAKE 104
SOUR CREAM CHOCOLATE ICING 104

CANDIES
CHOCOLATE CRUNCH 105
CHOCOLATE-PEANUT BUTTER
   CLUSTERS 105
CHOCOLATE COVERED POTATO CHIPS 105
CHOCOLATE DIPPED STRAWBERRIES 105
FUDGE 106
FUDGE FABULOUS 106
GUMDROP CANDY 106
HAYSTACKS 106
MARSHMALLOW CHOCOLATES 107
MARSHMALLOW TREATS 107
MILLIONAIRES 107
PEANUT BRITTLE 108
PEPPERMINT BARK 108
TINGLY CANDY 108
TURTLES 108

PIES
CRUMB CRUST 109
CHOCOLATE PIE 109
CHOCOLATE PECAN PIE 109
LIGHT AS A CLOUD CUSTARD PIE 110
EASY SUNDAE ICE CREAM PIE 110
SOUR CREAM LEMON OR LIME PIE 110
IMPOSSIBLE PUMPKIN PIE 111
PUMPKIN PECAN PIE 111
CHEESECAKE TARTS 111

OTHER SWEETS
APPLE CRISP 113
APPLE CHEESE CRISP 113
FRUIT CRUMBLE 114
FRUIT COBBLER 114
PEACH COBBLER 114
PEACH CRISP 115
BAKED CUSTARD 115
STRAWBERRIES AND CREAM TORTE 116
TAPIOCA PARFAITS 116

POTPOURRI
HOME MADE BROWNING FOR MEAT 117
BROWNING FOR PIE CRUST AND
   OTHER DOUGHS 117
BECHAMEL SAUCE 117
EGG SAUCE 117
FUDGE SAUCE 118
HOLLANDAISE SAUCE 118
HOT LEMON BUTTER 118

SAUCE IN A STICK 118
WHITE SAUCE 119
DOUGH ORNAMENTS 119
STRAWBERRY REFRIGERATED JAM 120
GARNISHES 120
DRYING HERBS 121
DRYING FRUITS AND VEGETABLES 121
DRYING LEAVES 121
DRYING FLOWERS 121
FLOWER TIME CHART 122
MISCELLANEOUS INFORMATION 123

C

For information

or

more copies of

"Definitive Microwave Cookery"

by

Carolyn Dodson

Please contact:
Carolyn Dodson
P.O. Box 8341
Wichita, Kansas 67208